3 Steps to Start-Up

Written for People New to Business

Steve Bridger
www.startuptosuccess.co.uk

Success
Before
Start-Up

Paperback ISBN 9781908218759
Mobipocket/Kindle ISBN 9781908218766
ePub ISBN 9781908218773

Published in the UK by MX Publishing 335 Princess Park Manor, Royal Drive, London, N11 3GX

A Vote of Thanks

A huge vote of thanks for the invaluable contributions made to *Success Before Start-Up* to all those who've shared their unique business experiences.

In featured order:

1. David Fernando and Andrew Marsh - The Best of Wimbledon & Merton and The Best of Kingston
2. Karen Badger - The Financial Management Centre
3. Tony Lemar – The Utility Warehouse
4. Mandy Robson – Herbalife
5. Joanne Waltham – babylovesshopping.co.uk
6. Richard Trussler – optimisemywebsite .co.uk
7. Tony Mingoia – Palazzo Restaurant
8. Kanu Patel and Vishnu Desai - The East Molesey Sub-Post Office
9. Matt and Tamsin Court - Belle Epoque
10. Neil Brand - Neil's Wheels
11. Trevor Marshall - Musicland East
12. Luigi Chiodaroli and Hilton Taylor - Elite Computing Solutions
13. Keith Grover – Freelance Writer
14. Karen Henfry – Chrysalis Family Wellbeing
15. Maria Morris – Ergonomic Consultant and Fuel the Soul
16. Stuart Amory – In-Kilter Fitness
17. Kevin Ring – Plasterhawks
18. Ray Thomas – Chemex Swindon

Special thanks also go to Professor Roy Seaman, co-founder and co-publisher of The Franchise Magazine. See page 29.

Dedication

This book is dedicated to Nooch for all her support and Annie, Brean, Jack, the Maries and not forgetting Mike and Barb Leeves.

CONTENTS

Success Before Start-Up

PREFACE

Success Before Start-Up
How to prepare for a new business
by
People who've done it
People just like you.

Relax. This is not another hefty book on business theory. All the help in the following pages has been drawn from:

- Insights from men and women who have put their hearts, souls and dreams into setting-up and running their own small businesses and…

- Solid advice learned the hard way from mistakes made and achievements celebrated and shared with you.

The intention is to pass on their knowledge and experiences to stop you making the same mistakes, under the umbrella theme of:
If only I knew then, what I know now

Success before Start-Up is a hymn to all those who have the courage and belief to step into the unknown and take those first faltering steps of going it alone. By passing on this knowledge, you'll be better equipped to anticipate problems, overcome setbacks, and, with hard work and dedication, be successful.

Businesses are the vehicles. People are the drivers.

You're reading this at the starting point, and no, the starting point is not when you start trading, but in the important months before, as you plan your future. This time is absolutely crucial as it should be used to focus your mind on two fundamental points:

First
Decide upon the kind of business you want to start

Second
Think about what you really want to achieve by running a business

Without sustained effort, your business will not pass the test of time. Starting is something that anyone can do. Keeping it going through the hard times demands dedication and strength of spirit.

Success Before Start-Up will help you make the right decisions for your future success.

We're with you – every step.

Introduction

The 3 Steps to Start-Up

The point of this book is to increase your chances of running a successful business. Many businesses fail in the first year, because they have not prepared for the challenges to come.

It's easy to get overwhelmed by all the legal and administrative red tape when you start thinking about starting a business. We understand that it can really put you off.

That's why *Success Before Start-Up* has been written in three sections so you can progress from one section to the next when you feel ready, knowing you can come back and refer to any point as many times as you like. The answer is to take it one step at a time, at your own pace. Before you know it, you'll be confident and well prepared.

The 3 Steps to Start-Up

- **Step 1** – Where you'll learn about 7 popular ways to start a business - and choose a way that suits you best. The big thing about this section is that you'll read true-life examples, from people like you who have begun businesses in each of the 7 most popular start-up options. They will be sharing their valuable personal experiences.

- **Step 2** – Having decided what route to take, Step 2 introduces The 4 Factors of Start-Up Success. The 4 Factors summarise the crucial elements you'll include in your business planning.

- **Step 3** – Pulls together all the different strands to help you prepare your first business plan -the plan you'll execute to start your own business.

Planning and preparation are the bedrocks of success

Here's a mantra to remember - The 5 Ps:
Proper Preparation Prevents Poor Performance

Recently, I visited a business start-up exhibition in London. It was full of people looking for a way to change their fortunes, a way to take more control of their lives, and a way to develop their talents for a better future.

There was enough energy and enthusiasm in that place to light up a small town.

Yet, 80% of those rushing off to the next seminar, or stuffing giveaway carrier bags with glossy brochures or speaking earnestly to business experts will fail.

They'll fail for one or more of these reasons:
- They had poor financial and management skills
- They overestimated demand for their product
- They were not ready to take on the challenge of opening a business
- They chose the wrong business
- They did not prepare

That's the negative bombshell being dropped. From this sentence onward, no more negativity. Forget about the 80% who don't make it. We want you to be among the 20% who do.

Success Before Start-Up will encourage you to develop your ideas and challenge them *before* you get involved in the whole legal, administrative and financial process of launching a new business. This will dramatically improve your chance of success.

Importantly, you can do this before you spend any serious money.

Head and Heart in Harmony

The ultimate aim when setting up your own business is to get your head and heart in harmony. So often, the heart powers ahead with high emotion and excitement to shape decision making. The head sometimes wakes up too late, only to find you've committed to something that's not right.

You want your heart to sing and your head to hum the tune.

These are the key pieces of advice from our team of small businesses:

- Do what you know, what you like and what suits your personality

- Do your research, understand the competition, make sure there's sufficient demand for your idea

- Try to fund your business from your own resources, avoid debt, and avoid bank loans if you possibly can

- Keep it tight. Don't spend what you haven't got. Expect low returns in the first year

- Remember that you have a life with family and friends outside the business; you'll need to unwind and relax to maintain your energy

Choose a way that suits you. Don't rush in

Going into business can be a gradual affair. You don't have to rush into anything or set up on your own from day one. Here's a perfectly good sliding scale of involvement to consider, for example:

Full-Time with a spare time twist

If you've got a job, stay in full-time employment, but add a new income stream in your spare time by getting involved in a business area that excites you.

This could be starting an online business. You could open an ebay or online shop, or adopt an MLM (multi-level-marketing) product and work from home.

Full-Time first, then go solo

Stay in full-time employment, improving your knowledge and skills, before you decide to go it alone in the same area of business.

This is an attractive option if you intend to offer your talents in a freelance service capacity – a graphic designer, IT specialist, marketing consultant, business coach, personal trainer, aromatherapist, reflexologist, stress coach, interior designer or whatever your skill base is that you can develop.

Part-Time working

If you have one job to pay the bills, take another that'll become your route to the future. The second job will allow you to get on-the-job training, gaining confidence and honing your skills. An example of this would be someone who takes a part-time job in a pub or restaurant, learning the ropes before they open their own place.

Take a franchise on a part-time basis

Switch from your main job when the franchise begins to grow. There'll be more details about franchising in a moment.

I want to start a business, but I don't know what kind of business

Remember that I was telling you about the business start-up exhibition? I was amazed when one of the exhibitors – it was a business coach – said that half the people who wanted to start a business had no idea what business it would be.

The desire was there, but not the direction.

To put that right, here are the most popular new business choices. A fuller description of each route will follow, along with real-life examples from people who have chosen that particular way of going into business. You'll then be in a much better position to shortlist the options that appeal to you most.

7 Popular Start-Up Options

Options	Short Description
1. Franchising	Franchising is when you buy into a successful business model to gain the benefits of a tried and tested concept with a proven track record. McDonald's, Subway, Sign-a-Rama, Baskin-Robbins, Ovenclean, Dyno-Rod, Molly Maid, Mr Electric and Safeclean are all examples of franchise opportunities. The total UK franchise market was valued at over £10 billion in 2009.
2. MLM	Multi Level Marketing is selling a successful product or service. The Utility Warehouse, Herbalife, Kleeneze, Avon Cosmetics and Forever Living are examples of well-known names.
3. Online Marketing	Buying or selling goods or services via the internet.
4. High Street Retail	Opening a retail outlet to promote your choice of products.
5. Professional and Trade Services	Directing your personal skills and talents and provide a service either working from home or from an office.

6. Buy an existing business	This option is a direct step to controlling an existing business by buying it outright. This approach may include buying a franchise re-sale.

Experience suggests that candidates 1-6 are less risky, but option 7 could change the world – just ask Sir James Dyson. There are many selling combinations and routes to market. For instance, you may have a high street shop with an e-commerce website to sell your shop products by mail order over the internet. You need to be imaginative to maximise your selling options.

7. New product Launch	The creation and launch of a totally new product or service. Then, setting up a business to promote and manage the idea.

The Start-Up Experience

The central issues that face a new business are pretty common to everyone, whether you're thinking of opening a retail shop or offering a trade or professional service.

Start-Up Stories provide a great source of helpful advice straight from people who went through the same stage you're going through now. Armed with this vital intelligence you will be better prepared to avoid mistakes and succeed.

Importantly, you'll realise that some quite different businesses have had similar experiences. There's a wealth of priceless knowledge in the following pages, all geared to your success.

Introducing the Start-Up Story Team

Business Sector	Business	Name	Type of Business
1. Franchise Page 24	The Best of Wimbledon & Merton and The Best of Kingston	Andrew Marsh David Fern ando.	Online business directory
2. Franchise Page 31	The Financial Management Centre	Karen Badger	Accountancy and financial services
3. MLM Page 40	Multi- Level Marketing The Utility Warehouse	Tony Lemar	Gas, electricity and phone utilities
4. MLM Page 45	Herbalife	Mandy Robson	Health and nutritional Products
5. Online Marketing Page 57	babylovesshoppping.co.uk	Joanne Waltham	Innovative products for babies
6. Online Marketing Page 61	optimisemywebsite.co.uk	Richard Trussler	Search Engine Optimisation
7. Online Marketing Page 65	Spanish Rings	Steve Bridger	International Mail Order

16

8. Running a Restaurant Page 73	Palazzo Italian Food with Passion	Tony Mingoia	Italian restaurant
9. Running a Post Office Page 77	Molesey Sub -Post Office	Kanu Patel	Local Post- Office
10. High Street Page 89	Belle Epoque Antiques for Modern Living	Matt and Tamsin Court	Antiques and stylish gifts
11. High Street Page 93	Neil's Wheels Bicycles Sales & Service	Neil Brand	New and second-hand cycles
12. High Street Page 97	Musicland East	Trevor Marshall	Instruments and in-shop tuition
13. Business Services Page 103	Elite Computing Solutions	Luigi Chiodar oli and Hilton Taylor	Computer repairs and Maintenance
14. Business Services Page 107	Freelance Writer	Keith Grover	Marketing copywriter
15. Business Services Page 115	Chrysalis Parental Coaching	Karen Henfrey	Family wellbeing consultancy

16. Business Services Page 118	Ergonomic & Cold Laser Consultant	Maria Morris	Ergonomics
17. Business Services Page 122	In-Kilter Fitness	Stuart Amory	Personal Trainer
18. Trade Services Page 126	Plasterhawks	Kevin Ring	Plastering
19. Buying a Business Page 132	Chemex Franchise Resale	Ray Thomas	Cleaning
20. New Product Launch Page 140	Spanish Rings Spanish style flowerpot holders	Steve Bridger	Gardening

Prime Pieces of Advice:

- Steer clear of debt
- Do your research
- Offer something different and appealing
- Provide a friendly personal service
- Be flexible and prepared to change if your original ideas are not working out.

First -Take the Tick Box Test

Taking the Tick Box Test will help you choose your start-up option. The test will highlight some of the characteristics you'll need, including strength of purpose, perseverance, positivity and passion. For the fun of it, you could ask someone who'll be objective, to match your answers for a second opinion.

	Yes	Usually	No
Score these points for each column:	**3**	**2**	**1**
1. Are you a confident and optimistic person?			
2. Do you have a strong desire for success?			
3. Do you stick at it to get results?			
4. Do you enjoy making decisions?			
5. Are you willing to wait for success?			
6. Do you enjoy putting your ideas across?			
7. Do you ask for advice from others?			
8. Are you prepared to learn new skills?			
9. Are you prepared to change your lifestyle?			
10. Are you willing to make sacrifices?			
11. Do you have the support of your family?			
12. Do you like being in control?			
13. Do you love it as your ideas come to life?			
14. Do you learn from mistakes and setbacks?			
15. Do you have an inner dynamo?			
16. Can you cope with increased stress?			
17. Are you prepared to take risks?			
18. Can you work on your own?			
19. Can you delegate work to others?			
20. Are you a realist?			
Column Totals:			

Add the scores of all 3 columns together:

_____

How does your future add up?

If you've scored:

1. Between 50 and 60 points. Top scores. Get ready for Start-Up!

You've got what it takes to run your own business from start-up. From these high scores, you seem to have that positive mixture of passion, personality and the level of realism you'll need to succeed.

This is where the evaluation of your idea and the development of your business model begin. You must subject them to scrutiny and examine each element dispassionately, to test how they'll perform in a competitive commercial environment.

2. Between 39 and 49 points – Almost there, but are two brains better than one?

The signs are good, but you may need to improve your skills, get a bit of business coaching or link with someone whose talents make the total package better.

Two or more heads could greatly improve the chance of business success. Often, a financial brain working alongside a visionary brain - in sales, marketing or product development, for example, can be a winning combination.

The appreciation of what talents each person can contribute will build a team of considerable strength and ability. There'll be times of exultant highs, countered by drawbacks and flat spots. It's during the difficult times when having help the support of others will be a tremendous benefit.

3. Between 28 and 38 points – Taking the inside track

Starting your own business from scratch is demanding. You could explore buying into an existing business to take a stake, or buy it outright.

This inside track route is an option if:
- You're a victim of redundancy
- The firm you work for is to be sold and you could take control in an MBO (Management buy-out)
- You want reassurance and proven performance provided by an existing business.

4. Between 20 and 27 points – Improve your skills and plan for the future

In the short term, you could opt for working in an area which interests you, gaining experience and developing your skills, before setting up your own business. Perhaps the time is not right now, but could be in the future.

Getting further training in your chosen field may help you decide on the right approach. Often people continue to work in their day job to fund future projects, switching over from one to the other when the time is right. It's not a bad plan to get a part-time job. This tactic is a good way of seeing what it's really like to work in a particular industry, rather than having the inaccurate view of an outsider.

Choosing the way forward

The following pages will provide an introduction to the 7 options in turn. You'll meet real people who have set up their own businesses in the different areas. The idea is to help you narrow down the contenders with most appeal, before conducting your own detailed research of your favourite route.

Here's an introduction to one of the fastest growing options on the market today – franchising.

Popular Start-Up Options
1
Franchising

Buying a Franchise

Buying a franchise gives your commercial plans a head start, by adopting an already successful business model. There's a lot to be said for opting for the franchise route, but you need to thoroughly research any opportunity.

A franchisor is the business rights owner of the concept and operation. A franchisee is someone who buys the licensed rights from the franchisor to operate the business in a particular location for an agreed period of time. A franchisee can also be referred to as the franchise owner. A financial investment gives you a ready-made business package.

Broadly speaking, there are two types of franchise structure.

1. **Business Format Franchising** - where full training is provided along with use of trademarks and a complete system of doing business, to include hiring and training staff, site selection, shop fitting and design plus advertising and marketing support. McDonald's, Burger King, Subway and Domino's Pizza are examples of business format franchising. Be aware that a substantial financial investment is required to take on a major high street name like McDonald's or Burger King.

    At the time of writing (January 2011) to open a McDonald's restaurant could cost from £125,000 - £325,000, with a requirement of at least 25% in unencumbered funds required from the potential franchisee. A franchisee would also be expected to have a healthy financial reserve for working capital.

2. **Product and Trade Name Franchising** – The key contribution here is the product or service to be sold, with the franchisee taking on the identity and branding and acting as the official representative of the parent company. Trademarks and logos are provided along with advertising, sales and marketing support. The business investor buys the products from the brand name company (the franchisor) and sells them to interested parties. This type of operation is well established in the automotive and soft drink markets. Snap-on Tools, Safeclean, Apollo Blinds and Lasertech are examples of product-based franchises.

The options are many and varied. Some have a low starting cost others may call for an investment of thousands plus a sizeable working capital provision.

Explore franchise candidates that:
- appeal to you and suit your personality
- are in high demand
- have little or no direct competition.

When considering franchise candidates, take a totally dispassionate stance. See what's missing in your locality, and then identify the product or service that will fill that demand gap and has the potential for future business growth.

It's essential that you conduct a thorough due diligence examination of any potential franchisor. Having said that, one of the main attractions of buying into a franchise is the prestige and importance of the brand you're buying into, and the solidity of the supporting company. The franchisor has spent a great deal of time and money establishing a brand identity, along with all the legal, marketing and organisational elements that have contributed to its success - success that you're buying into.

Start-Up Story Format

Each story follows the same format. Key pieces of advice - really useful nuggets of information - are introduced first, followed by a little background on each business to set the scene. The mid-section concentrates on what the businesses learned from start-up to the present day. The last section is where you'll read some final pieces of advice, as they take a last look back to leave you with important tips to help shape your success.

To give you a first taste of business in the real world, here's our first 'Start-Up Story'. It's been written with Andrew Marsh and David Fernando who opted for a business directory and networking franchise. Karen Badger who chose a totally different franchise model in accountancy will follow.

Afterwards, we'll return with some more information on the basics of franchising. Interestingly, you'll see that even though they are different franchise models, there are similar lessons to be learned.

Now for our first Start-Up Story.

**The Best of Wimbledon and Merton. The Best of Kingston
Andrew Marsh and David Fernando**

"Do what you know."

Key Advice

- Choose a franchise that suits your talents, interests and business background – it must complement your skills and your personality
- Research carefully to ensure your franchise makes commercial sense for your available resources – don't overstretch your finances
- Expect a full training programme – both initially and on-going - with supporting marketing material. Will you have a local area mentor?
- Confirm that 'back office' tools and systems are available to help you manage your new franchise – the more automated the process the better

- Double check the licence fee and commission system to calculate the true franchisee running costs
- Treble check the growth potential – with no 'me-too' franchises in your locality to hamper development
- Explore the performance incentives to reward your hard work

Background

Andrew and David worked for the same company in the media and magazine publishing industry. Having built up a solid level of trust and understanding, they decided to go into business together. The only problem was that they did not know what 'business' that was going to be. Purely by accident, a friend introduced them to The Best Of. At the time The Best Of was a basic online local business directory. With their experience, they envisioned not just an online directory, but a hugely exciting online magazine with considerable advertising, sponsorship and promotional potential.

Onward & Upward

The Best Of is zoned by local government boroughs. In May 2006, David and Andrew acquired the franchise for The Best of Merton (the precursor of The Best of Wimbledon and Merton). In July 2008, the Royal Borough of Kingston upon Thames was added to their holding. Nationally, The Best Of organisation is one of the fastest growing franchises with over three hundred sold.

The Best Of concept has developed as they have grown. The online community directory is still the centrepiece of activity, but now businesses can take advantage of numerous additional products and services, including print media, regular networking meetings, events and exhibitions, to promote themselves and gain new customers. By the same token, each of these events provides an opportunity to strengthen the business base and membership of their own franchises. The whole proposition becomes a mutually advantageous win-win concept. Andrew and David have grown the business from zero to 400 businesses, with numbers increasing as I write.

Is The Best Of Right for You?

This piece began with Andrew's quote "Do what you know". If you know sales, are outgoing, personable and enjoy mixing with a wide range of people then The Best Of could be for you. You'll need to make your own mark to build business and maintain the gains you've made. Everyone is given the same tools to be confident front of house and run an efficient back office. The Best Of is not a fast track to riches. It requires dedication and daily attention.

An attractive feature of The Best Of is that the annual licence fee is fixed on the perceived value of the holding as a geographical unit and not linked to income generation. This rewards hard work, as once the fee has been covered the balance remains with the franchisee.

Parting Pointers

The Best of Wimbledon and Merton won The Merton Business Award for Best Business for Marketing 2010 in recognition of what David and Andrew had achieved.

Looking back over the last four years, these are their parting thoughts:

- Be certain that your choice of franchise suits your experience, interests, skills and personality
- Maintain your enthusiasm and optimism to drive sales
- Ask for help and advice, and keep up to date with system developments
- Be flexible and make positive changes to your business plan – learn from other franchise owners
- Remember 'people buy people'. Your commitment and willingness to promote your clients' business will benefit your business
- Savour the social interaction
- Enjoy it

Andrew and David on 0208 286 2082
www.thebestof.co.uk/wimbledon-and-merton
www.thebestof.co.uk/kingston

Franchise Notes

What a Franchise Owner Should Expect from a Franchisor

To repeat, the term franchisor is the organisation that owns the brand property and has created the ready-made business model.

The franchise owner, (or franchisee) is the person who buys the licence rights to market the brand and replicates the business model in an agreed territory for a given length of time.

The process of franchising is the linking of these two parties for mutual benefit. The franchisor benefits from extending his reach in terms of the physical distribution of his business model. The franchisor receives an initial payment for selling the licence rights and thereafter will normally receive an annual fixed fee or a percentage of sales from the franchise owner.

The franchise owner has to have sufficient funds to cover the initial cost of license rights; this may be in the form of an upfront payment of 'say' 25%, with the balance being available as a loan from the franchisor at preferential rates, or from banks and other financial lenders.

Clearly, it's in the best interests of both parties to help each other as much as they can, but what should a franchise owner expect as a minimum when he takes on a new franchise?

Minimum Franchise Elements

- Nationally or even internationally known brand, with proven consumer/trade demand
- Clear and unambiguous licence terms to define franchise territory and agreement period
- Access to signage, plus sales and marketing support
- Full initial training for both product and business operation
- Access to on-going training and any free or payment terms for future training
- Back-office business support systems
- Details of financial status and track record of franchisor
- Evidence of a profitable business model

What a Franchisor will Expect

Buying a franchise is a contractual agreement. A franchise owner does not have the total freedom of someone creating their own business from scratch; they will have to agree to abide by a set of guidelines.

A franchise owner would be expected to follow:

1. The legal guidelines to promote and protect the brand image and product performance.
2. The operational processes and methodology developed by the franchisor
3. The high standards of quality and supervision

Furthermore, there would be a clause that restricts a franchise owner setting up a similar business in competition to the existing franchisor when the agreement expires.

Points a Franchise Agreement must include:

- A description of exact training and support offered
- Precise price, commission and rental fees involved
- Precise boundaries of the franchise territory
- Obligations to the franchisor
- Rights to renew or extend beyond original term
- Rights to sell/transfer ownership of the franchise
- Terms & Conditions for terminating contract
- Heir's rights in the event death

Franchise Expert Input

"Franchising is booming in the recession and is likely to become the most successful method of business expansion at both national and international levels in the future."

Professor Roy Seaman of The Franchise Magazine

As I began to write this section of the book, I had the good fortune to make contact with Professor Roy Seaman of 'The Franchise Magazine'. The monthly magazine is a mine of information on franchising with articles, reviews and directory pages. It's well worth getting hold of a copy or visiting their website if you want to explore the franchise opportunity in greater depth: www.thefranchisemagazine.net

Towards the back of the magazine is a checklist page that I particularly liked. The page is a valuable aid to decision making. It captures in 'bullet-point form' the pithy questions to ask a franchisor about their business and outlines the areas a franchise owner should consider when preparing their own business plan.

Two sections jumped out at me. The first was an eight-point summary on the elements a franchise agreement must cover. The second was astute advice for the unwary to identify a franchisor who may not be all they claim to be and should be avoided at all costs.

I am grateful to 'The Franchise Magazine' for giving permission to reproduce them here.

2. Be wary if the franchisor..........

- Tries to get you to sign a deposit agreement to reserve a territory
- Does not offer an automatic right to renew your agreement
- Has a very short-term contract
- Pressures you to 'act now' before the cost goes up
- Tries to trade you up to a higher fee
- Promises huge profits with thin investments
- Promises 'easy sales'
- Promises profits by sub-franchising
- Promises a large income working from home
- Fails to give statistics on sales and profits

- Evades identifying directors or principals
- Has no data on financial track record
- Cannot give plans on future development
- Has an incomprehensible contract or vague territories
- Is vague about support and training
- Has a name similar to a well- known business
- Is ignorant of competition
- Avoids detailing your financial obligations
- Tries to meet only in a hotel or has poor head office premises
- Is evasive about access to the existing franchise owner/s

www.thefranchisemagazine.net
email: enquiries@fdsltd.com

Franchising
Bookkeeping and Accountancy
Karen Badger

The Financial Management Centre Franchise

"Training, guidance, back-office systems, sales and marketing, these are some of the benefits of a franchise. You're not alone."

Key Advice

- Remember the words "You don't know what you don't know"- if you take on a franchise you will have people around you who are committed to your success. It is in their interest to give you all the support and training you need.
- Be realistic. Take off those rose-tinted glasses. Hope for the best, but make minimum projections of income for the first year
- Be prepared financially and mentally to cover those first hard yards before you become established
- Maximise your strengths, but get assistance in areas of weakness. Gather good people around you and don't be afraid to ask for advice
- Adopt a serious business mind-set – to make a franchise work it requires full-time commitment
- Be punctual, reliable and professional – but you know that.

Background

Karen has been involved with numbers since she was twelve years old and living in Cape Town. Her school was way ahead of its time by putting accountancy on the curriculum. Karen's early career was directed toward financial administration including the role of Deputy Finance Manager with the John Lewis Partnership in Reading.

Leaving John Lewis, she moved into greater financial control positions in the healthcare industry, first with Capio Healthcare and latterly in private hospitals, owned by Ramsey the Australian group. This was invaluable experience as she was liaising with heads of departments in a regional management capacity, preparing the monthly profit and loss accounts along with hospital management accounts. All this was perfect preparation for her franchise with The Financial Management Centre.

Choosing Her Franchise

From reading the last paragraph, you'll appreciate that someone with Karen's experience would not make an important franchise decision without completing a due diligence exercise on the various bookkeeping and accountancy franchises available.

These are some of the reasons why Karen chose The Financial Management Centre (TFMC):

- It is managed by a young team of innovative thinkers willing to listen to feedback and provide personal support for new members
- They arrange 'Discovery Days' for potential members, where they conduct one to one meetings to answer any questions and give advice
- They respect your ability as a bookkeeper - the aim being to make you a more successful one
- The franchise offers a flexible triple entry plan. The TFMC organises their franchise territories by geographical area. Level 1 is the lowest upfront cost for the basic franchise with 3 guaranteed business leads; level 2 has 13 business leads. The third 'Fast Growth' level has 20+ business leads.
- Once you select the Level of your choice there is a franchise payment to be made. Thereafter, a percentage commission is paid annually
- Full training is given, along with sales and marketing support to include your own local website. Karen estimates that 40% of her new business is generated through the web.

Parting Points

If you're thinking of starting a bookkeeping and/or accountancy franchise, here are Karen's last words of advice:

- Do your research on your local area to assess the competition and to find the right franchise for your situation
- When checking out the local competition, ring them and ask for their rates. Set your own hourly rates with this knowledge
- Halve your income forecast for the first 6 months and revise your business plan accordingly
- Work hard to maintain the loyalty of existing clients
- Gear up any new business drive from the beginning of the New Year. Businesses may like to hear from you in the run up to the April year-end and from May onwards, when they may want a new accountancy arm if dissatisfied with the service they're getting now
- From your experience as a bookkeeper, feedback any financial warning signs to your clients – especially new businesses who are just starting out

Karen Badger
The Financial Management Centre Leatherhead and Kingston
T: 01372 700120
Karen.badger@tfmcentre.co.uk
http://leatherhead.tfmcentre.co.uk
http://kingston.tfmcentre.co.uk

Parting Points on Franchising

Undeniably, franchising is an appealing option for those who have sufficient funds from savings, redundancy, inheritance or loans. Liquid cash will be required to support the franchise purchase and supply the essential working capital. Further financial provision will definitely be needed for personal use to keep the wolf from the door as you enter a training and set-up period.

The variety of franchises on offer increases all the time, from the simple to the complex, from the relatively inexpensive to ones quoted in many thousands. Here are some tips to help you develop your plans:

1. Draw up a shortlist of candidates and attend open days to learn more about the detailed workings of the franchise.
2. Run the rule over the financial figures to calculate the total cost of the franchise and anticipated 'ROI' - return on investment. Prepare a min/max turnover and profit and loss statement for your business plan, along with a realistic estimate of working capital required. Armed with this information, you can write you own business plan. Be realistic in terms of turnover and profit for the first year.
3. Ask permission to speak to other franchise owners – and value their feedback.
4. If you've had no previous experience in recruiting and managing employees, ask for extra training to span both the legal, tax and employee relations aspects.
5. Go onto the internet or get hold of franchise magazines to find specialist consultants who can give you specially tailored advice on choosing, launching and running your chosen franchise.

Thorough preparation at this stage is vital. Money spent on education, research and advice will pay you back handsomely.

For more information on franchising contact:
The British Franchising Organisation http://www.thebfa.org/
The Franchise Magazine -www.thefranchisemagazine.net

MLM – What is it?

MLM (multi-level-marketing) also called network marketing, affiliate marketing or direct selling is a flexible way to create a second part-time income stream that has the potential to develop into a full-time business occupation.

People who join MLM sales operations do so on a self-employed basis and are therefore responsible for managing their own tax matters. After paying a joining fee and completing a training period, new members become known as Independent Distributors. Remuneration is directly related to their sales performance and to the performance of people who join their sales team. The whole concept of MLM depends upon word of mouth, with distributors selling to individuals who subsequently join the sales effort and become members of their team.

MLM is a legitimate marketing technique that rewards sales effort by creating layers of activity, triggered in the first instance by one person making one sale. A downward cascade of sales starts to flow when others are recruited and begin selling the same products to their contacts. More contacts recruit more people with the process growing ever wider and bigger. In your mind, visualise a triangular shape with you at the top of your own group of contacts. They're laid out below with your recruits forming the ever-widening layers you as the organisation grows.

The incentive is that everyone involved in the exercise from the first person to the newest recruit, benefit from the sales activity. The first person receives commission not only from generating his own personal sales, but also receives a small percentage of sales made by all the people connected with him.

Here's a visual representation of a classic MLM structure that shows the way people join the network you've created and how it expands and duplicates itself. Imagine you are the black figure at the top of the triangle. You've recruited two people who in turn recruit two more, ultimately building a network of fifteen people including yourself. Due to the multiplier effect of this model, if each member of your network follows the same pattern by recruiting two distributors the total network has the potential for massive growth.

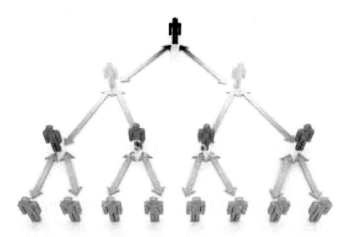

Up-line and Down-line

The person who recruited you to the operation is called your 'up-line' and all those recruited subsequently by yourself are called the 'down-line'. The way to generate a substantial income is to expand the down-line. Remuneration flows with every sale made. The harder you work, the more time you commit, the more the rewards. This is why MLM as a business model is a flexible part-time option that can grow and allow you to cross over into a full-time commitment.

The Value of Up-line Support

You'll receive training, supporting literature and business manuals from your chosen MLM company. At first, you may be understandably nervous about speaking to people in a sales capacity, especially if this is something you're not used to. The most important thing is to be yourself, have confidence in the product or service and speak from your own product experience. Building an MLM business is about building relationships and trust.

This is why it is imperative that you get solid, reliable hands-on support from the person who first introduced you to the opportunity. Expect them to accompany you on your first trips to help and guide you in the sales process. MLM sales are a person-to-person exercise, so no hard sell. Try to be relaxed and professional at the same time. Being successful in the first couple of sales will be enough to give you confidence to fly solo. Having an active mentor will pay dividends. It's in your up-line's interest for you to be successful, but it's up to you to keep abreast of new product developments and attend regular meetings and group training sessions.

MLM does take time to build and is not a path to instant riches. Some people, like Tony Lemar, whose story you'll read shortly, looked upon the opportunity as a pension plan to run alongside his day-job. Others who were in a position to devote more time to their chosen MLM managed to generate enough income to be able to switch to work full-time and leave their past employment behind.

MLM and Pyramid Selling. One is an Illegal Scam - but Which One?

I need to clarify something before going any further. There's confusion about MLM being mistaken as an illegal pyramid selling scheme. Let me explain the differences.

An Illegal Pyramid Scam

A pyramid selling scheme requires unwitting people to pay money upfront on the pretext that they'll share in a golden jackpot of cash or goods created by other people being enrolled and 'investing' money as well. The thing is that there is no jackpot and no products or services involved. Pyramid schemes work like a financial chain letter that promise payment but never deliver. They are a scam. A fraud.

A Legal Multi-Level-Marketing Operation

MLM companies do have products or services that can be seen, touched, bought and sold in the conventional way. Companies like Avon Cosmetics, Herbalife, Tupperware and Forever Living Aloe Vera products have ranges of products that people can sample and decide to buy if satisfied with the quality and price.

Crucially, it is when someone is delighted with the product, has confidence in the sales person, and is sure they're dealing with a reputable company that they may decide to become sales agents and independent distributors themselves.

You will find that most MLM brands do not have a large consumer media budget, to advertise on television, for example. The media budget is directed at promoting their wares through their distribution network, with regular training and sales incentives geared to reaching and surpassing sales targets.

MLM Business Model - The Utility Warehouse Discount Club

The Utility Warehouse Discount Club offers telephone, gas and electricity utility services at a discount price to people who become club members. Their business model is to purchase telephone and utility services direct from the supplier at wholesale prices. The benefit of becoming a club member is reduced prices below that of the 'Big 6' utility operators, like British Gas and the regional electricity boards.

The Utility Warehouse Discount Club offers a range of mobile phones to members, but their operation is primarily geared to providing different basic services, for example:
- Lower cost telephone line rental and call costs
- Broadband for calls and internet connection
- Cheaper gas and electricity

The company performs well in consumer tests and regularly achieves the 'Best Buy' status with the magazine 'Which?' Club members also benefit from using a cashback card that can be used in a range of high street shops and for services. Members add cash to their cards online or via the telephone. When they do their weekly shop and pay using the cash on their cashback card they earn a 5% discount on their Utility Warehouse monthly invoice.

Tony Lemar chose the Utility Warehouse, this is his story.

MLM
The Utility Warehouse Discount Club

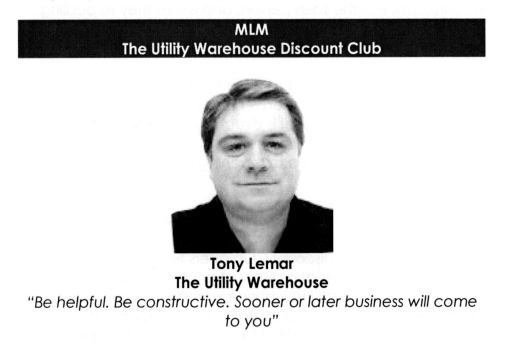

Tony Lemar
The Utility Warehouse
"Be helpful. Be constructive. Sooner or later business will come to you"

Key Advice

- Explore a number of MLM opportunities before you commit yourself
- Make sure there's sufficient demand for the chosen product or service you've chosen
- If you opt for a product, don't tie up capital with slow moving stock
- Expect on-going training and support to develop sales and create your own network
- Be sure you've chosen a reputable concern with a successful track record. Do your 'due diligence' checks. MLM is a legal trading scheme where goods or services are legitimately sold. Beware of illegal pyramid selling schemes
- Be prepared to work at it – building your network and gaining rewards takes time

Background

Tony has been self-employed for most of his professional career as an IT consultant. He began as a computer operator and programmer specialising in bespoke business software solutions. Over the years, he has worked in Australia and been involved with many blue-chip companies in the UK. Today, Tony defines his role as an Enterprise Architect helping companies improve their business processes by implementing software and hardware IT solutions.

Multi-Level-Marketing with the Utility Warehouse Discount Club

Five years ago, Tony decided to research the franchise and MLM markets to establish a second income stream. He wanted something that would sit side-by-side with his IT consultancy, would be flexible and have the potential of future growth. The Utility Warehouse ticked all those boxes.

The Utility Warehouse is the trading name of Telecom Plus PLC a FTSE listed company with an annual turnover in excess of £360 million.

The company is a re-seller of basic utilities – gas and electricity, mobiles, phone and broadband packages. The company doesn't spend money on expensive advertising campaigns. Instead, it relies on personal recommendation by satisfied customers and distributors telling others about the company. The Utility Warehouse passes the savings it makes on to its members by charging less for its services.

The Utility Warehouse business model attracted Tony to become a distributor because of:

- Low investment cost to start a Utility Warehouse business
- Free training and on-going distributor support
- No stock to buy – upfront or at any time
- High demand for a product range everyone needs and uses
- Share option scheme with an established PLC
- Flexible working – part-time or full-time as suits your situation
- The freedom to work from home
- Potential to build a team and directly benefit from their sales performance
- On-going residual income from sales. Residual income means that you continue to benefit from a percentage of the sale value each time a sale is made. In the case of the Utility Warehouse, every time a customer uses any product – turns on a light, uses the gas, makes a phone call - you receive a share of the sale value as a payment based on a percentage of the customer's monthly utility bill.

MLM Team Building

MLM relationships are between self-employed individuals, responsible for their own personal tax, and their chosen 'host' company. These individuals are usually given the title of Official Distributors. Building a successful MLM business means building a successful team; this is how the structure works:

1. In the beginning, Tony worked to find and introduce customers to the Utility Warehouse. He is paid commission generated by these customers.
2. The second stage is for some of his customers, who had enjoyed making savings from their monthly bills, to join Tony as part of his distributor team. Tony now has a mix of personal customers and customers who have become distributors.
3. The third stage is for Tony's new distributors to introduce their own fresh contacts as customers, some of whom will become distributors.

An ever-growing tree continues to flourish. The concept is based on first-time customers gaining the benefits and being satisfied with the Utility Warehouse service. By sharing this experience by word-of-mouth they create a new extended network.

Parting Points

If you are thinking of exploring the world of MLM, these are some points from Tony to bear in mind:

- Your success is largely dependent upon your own commitment and involvement. It's up to you to put in the hours to gain the rewards

- Choose a product or service with wide appeal – MLM is a numbers game and if you select a niche product with limited appeal, you will cut down your chance of success
- Pick the right dedicated people to join your team – you need a reliable group of people that pull in the same direction
- 64% of people get work from people they know and who like and trust them
- Build relationships through business and social networking to enhance your profile
- Avoid the hard sell – have confidence in your chosen product or service

Tony Lemar
Independent Distributor
The Utility Warehouse
M: 0780 253 1632
tonylemar@uwclub.net
www.lowcostutilities.co.uk

MLM – A marketing system that's stood the test of time

The most successful MLM companies have been established for a number of years and have developed their product range, business organisation and training programme to maximise returns. Amway, the USA leader, has been established for 51 years, Herbalife for 30 years and Forever Living for 32 years. Avon Cosmetics is entering its 53rd year in 2011. Tupperware has been holding their famous parties for 60 years. You can share the rewards from this system of business operation if you're willing to put in the hard yards at the beginning. Once you've created a critical mass of sales fed by a combination of your own personal sales and income generated by your down-line, then you should expect to see your total income really take off.

MLM - Network Marketing
Herbalife Products

Mandy Robson
Personal Wellness Coach
Herbalife International Independent Distributor
Nutrition & Health Products

"I help people improve their lifestyle, be healthier, fitter, enabling them to stay away from the doctor and make the most of their lives."

Key Advice

- You have to be a self-starter, with drive and determination, to be successful in an MLM business.
- Choose a company with a proven range of products and experience in organising and managing this type of direct selling operation.
- As an ambassador of the company, you need to be totally convinced, through your own personal experience, of the quality and effectiveness of the products you have on offer. So, if you use the products, you'll sell them with conviction.
- Selling to people directly is a one-to-one experience – your customers 'buy' you when they buy the products. You have to be professional, knowledgeable and don't

be pushy. Often, people need time to think before making a decision; provide them with the benefits and let them decide.

- Gain in-depth product knowledge through training and your own efforts. Look for ways to introduce the product benefits to different selling situations and sectors.
- Make sure the financial remuneration reflects your level of commitment and own business plan. You need to believe in the company's marketing plan and bring it to life in your own business situation.
- The more you learn about the company you choose, the more excited you should become about the potential for future rewards.

Background

After working for a major corporate company for over twenty years, Mandy became a victim of downsizing. When the threatened axe did fall, it was the signal to start a new chapter in her life - a chapter where she was in control and not controlled.

Her involvement with Herbalife somehow seemed preordained. A chance introduction to their range of health and nutritional products coincided with her own determination to recover her fitness. She began sampling the products and taking more exercise. The positive combination of both was the proof that she should explore Herbalife as a serious business opportunity.

Herbalife – The Trading System

For over 30 years, Herbalife has developed a range of scientifically proven nutritional and health products. The products fall into four categories: weight management and core nutrition, sports and performance, targeted nutrition and outer nutrition. Independent distributors have the freedom to represent the company within the UK and internationally to whoever wishes to purchase the products to benefit their personal wellbeing.

Distributors take orders from customers, purchase the required products from Herbalife at wholesale prices, and then sell on to customers at the full retail price. Their remuneration is the margin between wholesale and retail prices, which is a minimum '25%' increasing to 50%.

As a distributor grows their business and attains the level of supervisor, they have the ability to introduce and manage their own network of distributor recruits, who generate additional remuneration of royalties and bonus payments. Herbalife holds regular monthly training meetings in London, Birmingham, Manchester and Dublin. Free online training is available via UK and international webinar conferencing.

The Sales Effort

Having sampled the products and completed her training, Mandy started by approaching the market using the simplest and most successful technique of all – just talking to people! She hosts Herbalife parties, takes space at various wedding and wellbeing events and local health and fitness centres. At these events Mandy carries out body fat testing and offers 12- Week healthy weight loss classes, with the aim of educating people of the importance of nutrition and how they can achieve a balanced lifestyle.

At wedding and wellbeing events, she concentrates on weight control, core nutritional and outer nutrition products, to support chosen lifestyle goals. The focus shifts to sports performance, energy and muscle gain nutrition in a gym or sporting environment. Muscle gain, body fat reduction, protein intake and related aspects of health and fitness are supported by Herbalife research, product trials and scientific testing.

Mandy sensitively selects the most appropriate combination of products for her clients. Ongoing coaching is critical to ensure the products have been used as recommended to achieve the agreed goals. As Herbalife products are not available in high street shops, word-of-mouth recommendations are extremely important, but there are other strands to building her business as well.

Networking Gains

www.idealwellbeing.com is Mandy's internet shop window and e-commerce sales channel. The website reinforces her one-to-one activities and provides an alternative way for her customers to order products and for people who search for Herbalife products to buy online.

Joining a business networking group presents new opportunities. She attends a regular breakfast networking group with the prospect of further sales. Additionally, it is a way of developing her business skills. Business networking connects her with a source of advice as other like-minded small business owners are willing to share their experiences. Mandy has also developed a rewarding internal network with fellow Herbalife distributors to learn and share ideas for mutual benefit. This has proved to be of real benefit as it encourages team working and mutual support.

Parting Points

Mandy is building her business on strong foundations. Here are some parting words of advice:

- This may surprise you, but you don't need to have past experience in sales or be a 'salesy' extrovert to be an effective distributor.
- It doesn't help to pressure people to buy when you first start. If they're keen, they'll buy immediately – keep in touch and your professionalism will create respect for your recommendations and referrals.
- Planning is central to creating an effective business and you should have a 90-day plan.
- Read the local press for events or group meetings you think will be receptive to your messages.
- Keep a note of events you've attended. Prepare a written record of how successful they were and of potential improvements or changes you'd make for future events.
- Learn from experience to improve your performance and pass that knowledge onto your future down-line.
- Get yourself connected online with your own website and email contact list.
- Build awareness and business skills through networking events and using social media, for example Facebook, Twitter and LinkedIn.
- Accept that it will take time and effort to get established. Keep positive, especially in those early months when you're just starting out.
- Be prepared to try a different approach that has worked for other distributors and learn from those who have grown a successful business and were once just like you.

Mandy Robson
M: 07968 309 168
idealwellbeing@virginmedia.com
www.idealwellbeing.com

Popular Start-Up Options
3
Online Marketing

A desk, a chair, a computer, an internet connection and you could be in business. This next section looks at the ways that you can become operational online to:

- Turn a hobby into a business

- Use your IT skills and knowledge of the internet to provide specialist help and support to businesses as a 'B2B' (business to business) or a 'B2C' (business to consumer) service

- Sell products via mail order or provide a service directly to customers online

But first, step back and look at the big picture...

Get excited! Think of your website as your own 'BBC' - Business Broadcasting Centre.

Imagine your website as a central control centre, your business communication hub. Your website has the capacity to become an internet radio and television station, hosting podcasts (audio recordings downloaded from your site) and 'You Tube'- type videos showing product demonstrations or sales pitches across the world. Consistent email marketing, blogging and articles will raise awareness and drive your business forward.

The internet has opened many possibilities to operate on a global scale. They are many ways to use the net to achieve your business aims. The entry point is the home page, the focal point of your marketing communications.

When you're preparing for launch, the design and function of a website must be at the top of your priority list. Your website is an amazing tool, but it needs to be designed to handle the tasks you want it to perform. Many sites are no more than online brochures to be visited by the few who have the web address.

Don't be put off by the technical nature of building and operating a website as there are talented people who will advise you on the best solution for your budget. Websites can be upgraded in a modular fashion to include fresh elements as your finances allow.

Going Online – Creating your Presence on the Internet

1. Domain Names – Your URL

A domain name is your internet address or URL (Universal Resource Locator). The domain name should be indicative of your business function and link with your business name. For example, www.virginatlantic.com is the domain name for Virgin Atlantic Airlines Limited. www.designer-software.co.uk is the domain name for Designer-software who specialise in creating bespoke business software. Domain names may be taken by a company purely as an indicator of the business sector they operate in –for example, www.wine.com and www.toys.com.

A suitable domain name for your business ideally has to be:

- Linked to the business function
- Short, so it can be easily remembered
- Easy to write down or type from a keyboard without confusion
- Without letters in the domain name that when viewed together create other short words with 'unfortunate' meanings

Jot down a shortlist of candidate names, log onto the internet and search for domain names and the page will come alive with a variety of companies that are accredited with ICANN (Internet Corporation for Assigned Names and Numbers). These companies for example, www.lowcostnames.co.uk, www.godaddy.com, www.names.co.uk , check and register names under the DNS (Domain Name System).

The domain name is completed by an identifying tag. There are many to choose from, the most popular are .com .co.uk .net, and .biz. There is a hierarchy of domain name tags with the ones most widely used across the internet .com and .co for example, costing more than geographically defined tags like .co.uk. Domain name registration is for a set period in time. Usually you can buy a name for your exclusive use from 1 year to 5 years before you'll be asked to pay to renew the name.

2. Hosting and Email

Once you've registered your preferred domain name, you're faced with the decision of how to make the name operational. Most domain name registration companies offer website and email hosting. The word 'host' means the renting of space on internet servers. You may have heard the term 'ISPs' (Internet Service Providers). An ISP is responsible for connecting your business to the internet.

If you want to establish your enterprise as a serious business, it's more impressive to use your domain name in the email title. To explain, you can get a free Yahoo or Hotmail email function for personal use (name@hotmail.com) or one linked to your broadband supplier with the cost of hosting the email function as part of the package (name@btinternet.com) or (name@virginmedia.com). However, if your domain name, email and website are hosted on an ISPs server you can then use your own business URL, for example, info@spanishrings.com

I use lowcostnames.co.uk to register and manage my domain names. My website is hosted by the web designer on his server. You don't have to use one company; you can choose the best combination to suit your needs.

3. Website Design and Creation

Even though we're surrounded by technical experts who speak fluent 'geek', in plain English, there are two major elements of website design to consider:

- The first is the build quality and functionality of your website
- The second is the on-going promotion of it – SEO for short (Search Engine Optimisation)

As you would expect, these two are inter-connected in that the 'mother-ship' of your website needs to have built into it the promotional communication software like blogs and social media.

I'll avoid getting too technical as I'm not a wizard in the 'dark arts' of website software, hardware and SEO (search engine optimisation). Shortly, you'll meet Richard Trussler of www.optimisemywebsite.co.uk , he's such an SEO wizard; he's even got a pointy hat with stars and moons on it.

Here's a breakdown of the features of website creation and promotion.

Design Elements

Website design has two strands: the technical functionality and the creative presentation of content. Content is the written word, pictures and visual style. Technical functionality uses HTML (Hyper Text Markup Language) - the code most widely used in the World Wide Web. The test of a successful website design is how well these two elements intertwine.

Never forget that a website must be created to attract, hold and convert visitors. They must be people-friendly, easy to use and interact with. Remember 'KISS' – Keep It Simple and Straightforward. There's not a lot of value in having a fabulously effective SEO and technical support structure, if when visitors arrive at your site, they find it hard to understand.

Major Design Features

The home page is the main landing page as visitors arrive at your website by clicking on your domain name. Research has shown an average stay on a website is no longer than seven seconds before moving off to the next.

That's why it's imperative that the home page provides the key text and visual messages to hold the visitor. Think of the home page doing the job of a large poster to make an impact and capture attention. If your visitor thinks they've found the right place, they'll stay and explore.

The home page is an advert for the rest of the site. It could also host links to both business and social networking sites like Linkedin and ecademy for business, and Facebook and Twitter for either social or business.

Beware of using Flash images on the home page. Flash can be used on supporting pages. Flash images are visual images that cannot be seen or read by search engines thus redundant as far as SEO is concerned.

Privacy policy, terms and conditions, postal address, landline phone numbers and comply with any regulatory or legal stipulations. Often these small print requirements are run along the base of the home page with the main page navigation tabs at the top of the page.
If your company is a UK Limited Company or an LLP (Limited Liability Partnership), under the Companies Act 2006 you

should feature within the website, not necessarily on the home page:

- the full name of the company or LLP
- the registered office address
- the registered company/LLP number
- the place or registration
- the VAT number if VAT registered

Simple and clear page navigation will route the visitor to where they want to go with links to other site pages. Some complex websites with many sub-sections or different services or products, featured in a site map. This is a schematic diagram of content on a separate page with links to all site pages.

A CMS (content management system) like Joomla for example, allows the site owner to enter and make text or visual changes. This avoids the expense of employing a web expert to make simple updates.

This is especially important with an e-commerce site. Spanishrings.com is an e-commerce site selling products via mail order. Take a look to see how the site is structured to provide information before explaining how to make an online purchase.

Prices, stock holding and product information can be updated in moments and immediately go live online. By the way, if you're selling online, make sure you feature reassurance about paying online with gold symbols of safes or locks, as well as credit and debit card logos.

Email and contact details should ideally be featured on every page. Most sites opt for a separate contact page, but as visitors often arrive or land on your site at a page other than the home page, it's helpful to adopt a belt and braces approach.

Blogs, podcasts, video, social media logos, email newsletters, links, backlinks and photo galleries are all indicators of how your business can be connected to your customers, followers, supporters and even customer relations critics. Interaction with customers builds a greater online presence. These are important tools to promote your business and communicate with potential customers. They allow you to add a human face to an internet existence; even if you receive a negative reaction or receive criticism, you can react and solve issues promptly.

I hope these last paragraphs have given you a taste for the huge potential that awaits you online. We'll return to websites later, as part of the overall marketing mix in Step 2 along with the Marketing Factor, and starting to prepare your first business plan.

In the meantime, let's continue with the advice from three online marketing businesses.

Turning a Hobby into a Business

The first is Baby Loves Shopping. Joanne Waltham began by buying and selling personal items on ebay. She took an increased interest in baby products and decided to test the market for innovative ideas to fulfil parents and babies with their individual needs. This is her story.

Online Marketing
www.babylovesshopping.co.uk

Joanne Waltham
www.babylovesshopping.co.uk
Innovative Baby Products

"As a 'mumpreneur', I wanted to provide other mums with a special service that understood their needs."

Key Advice

- It's possible to create an online business without spending a fortune – there are affordable website design templates with shopping cart software that won't break the bank
- Some companies will not supply their products to people who operate ebay shops – you may opt for creating your own website instead
- Make sure that you comply with the necessary legal requirements in terms of distance selling regulations, Data Protection Act and within your terms and conditions of Sale
- Set up an efficient fulfilment operation to deliver your products swiftly to customers
- Provide contact details so people can ask questions and get attention from a real person – not just via email. You need to provide help and reassurance to customers.

Background

Joanne was an IT manager. As a mother of two, she explored the baby product market to find the best products for her babies. She realised that, while there were thousands of different products to choose from, there was a scarcity of products from small companies at the cutting edge of innovation that were not stocked by the big high street shops.

Baby Loves Shopping was created to fill that gap in the market. Her website is a haven for mums looking for ingenious ideas that would make their lives easier and that most importantly their babies would love.

The Creation of Baby Loves Shopping

The creation of Baby Loves Shopping stemmed from a desire to run a business from home and create an income, while also being on hand to look after the children and attend to the needs of her wider family. As Joanne wanted to take the process step-by-step, she started as a sole trader on the basis that she could trade up to the status of a Limited Company and register for VAT as the company grew.

Her first trading days were as an ebay shop. However, some of her suppliers did not want to run the risk of seeming to devalue their brands by the ebay association. Primarily, this was because the image of the products and their premium positioning needed to be protected.

This led to Joanne setting up her own site to host her range of innovative products. The products she selected are delivered to a special warehouse that performs the important functions of storing, pick, pack and handling, and despatch to customers. By using a fulfilment service, she could keep her home life separate from the management of her online business.

The Buzz

Being able to introduce someone to a product that solves a problem gives Joanne a buzz. To know that selling something she's recommended has made a real difference, gives her an enormous sense of satisfaction. Providing advice and guidance underpins the commercial activity of Baby Loves Shopping. It's far more than a trading platform – it's a relationship of trust that creates a bond with her customers.

Parting Points

If you're exploring the online marketing option, these are some pointers from Joanne:

- Become an expert in a niche that has relevance to a large number of people
- Offer products with a range of price points to appeal to a wide audience
- Give help and advice to create a personal relationship with customers that even though it is an internet relationship
- Make sure you have maximum software protection especially in anti- fraud security
- Make use of social media and business networking to raise awareness of your business and gain valuable help and advice.

Joanne Waltham
T: 01784 409 732
sales@babylovesshopping.co.uk

Opening an ebay Shop – www.ebay.co.uk

ebay provides a thorough, speedy and efficient way to create your own designated online shop. ebay is used by many companies as either their primary or secondary sales channel. You will read of people who've had no experience of selling online, who began by selling a few personal items in a private capacity, then upgraded to a business account and changed their working lives by buying and selling goods through their ebay shop. ebay has an international reach of over 181 million customers with business conducted within UK borders and across the world, so the potential is huge. It is estimated that there are over 10,000 businesses selling through ebayUK alone.

To open an ebay shop you need to have at least 5 positive ebay buyer reviews. These will be achieved by using the basic auction format and getting excellent feedback scores. Once you have an ebay shop up and running you will have the added option of running products on a 'Buy it Now' basis that can be linked to an auction listing.

It is a simple process to get listed. All you need is a user name, password, along with a UK postal address and an email address to register. Fees are charged on a direct debit subscription basis and you will be required to open a PayPal account. For full details log on to www.ebay.co.uk, click on the sell tab and scroll down to the Business Centre option. You'll find all you need to know to get started there.

Creating an Online Specialist Consultancy Business

Selling your professional skills online is a realistic new business start-up option. Domain name registration and specialist IT services such as search engine optimisation can be accomplished remotely using only the computer, email and telephone to communicate with potential clients.
The human contact is made by phone after an initial approach is triggered by someone visiting your website or dropping you an email.

Specialists, like IT computer repair services, freelance copywriters, graphic designers and website designers, regularly respond to enquiries made by email that lead to a face-to-face meeting at a second stage. Recently, I completed a project by writing text for a website; the web designer I was working with was based in the Philippines!

I mentioned Richard Trussler the 'SEO magician' a few pages ago. This is his Start-Up Story:

Online Marketing
www.optimisemywebsite.co.uk
www.thesmallbusinessseocompany.co.uk

Richard Trussler
SEO Services and Online Marketing Consultants
"Never forget: your business is to help other businesses succeed."

Key Advice

- Always devote your expertise to the commercial benefit of your client
- It's the successful end result clients want, not to be dazzled by your technical prowess
- Understand the market your clients inhabit - use the language and search terms the market uses
- Get inside the heads of your client's customers to know what they want and what they're looking for – what makes them tick
- Track the route of how people found your client's website – gather this valuable information from customers

- Getting to No 1 on Google is NOT the aim. Getting to No 1 on Google with the RIGHT TRAFFIC is the aim!
- Analyse results – what is working and what is not, assess where's the best place for clients to spend their money

Background

Richard left school at sixteen, did his City and Guilds in Brickwork, Carpentry and Joinery and began working, as they say in the trade, 'on the tools'. That's probably not what you expected to read about for someone involved in such a sophisticated and highly technical industry as online marketing.

Then again, Richard is not your usual geeky computer whizz. He brings a refreshing no bull attitude to search engine optimisation. His past work experience has sharpened his business acumen and created a results-driven mentality that has proved successful in building his business.

Even at school, Richard was fascinated by computers. He was to return to them as a result of an accident. If you've read some of the other start-up stories, you'll know that unexpected events have changed the lives of other people too. At the time, Richard had set up a sub-aqua dive shop. He became an experienced diver and instructor. Unfortunately (or with hindsight, was it fortunately?) he had a recompression accident that changed his career path.

Y2K – Year 2000 when IT Changed Forever

Richard closed the dive shop and moved onto the next phase of his life. After attending Microsoft training courses, he was offered a job with Glaxo by a friend from his diving days. Most of his time was spent co-ordinating a large network of computers and users in preparation for 31st December 1999.

Y2K catapulted IT to the top of the business agenda and spawned the mighty industry it is today. After leaving Glaxo, Richard went on to work with the formation of Tesco.com where his previous experience in the building industry was an immense advantage. His combination of skills were in demand just as Tesco were expanding and building new outlets.

SEO to Now

It's amazing how luck can play an important role in our lives. Being involved with Tesco.com ten years ago was a spur to Richard learning website design skills. One of his first jobs was to build a website for a football correspondent of one of the national tabloids. The correspondent would put his predictions for match results online. Online betting was just kicking off and the website shot to the first page on Google with traffic numbers increasing every day. The traffic attracted advertisers with website banners for companies like Littlewoods and Vernon's' Pools. The arrival of two cheques from advertisers, one for £4,000 and one for £6,000, alerted them to the potential of monetising websites and the online tracking of visitor behaviour or search engine optimisation.

Gone Fishing

www.optimisemywebsite.co.uk offers online marketing strategy advice, as well as technical support. Richard's advice is to adopt a flexible budget spending strategy. 80% of the budget is devoted to areas that are known to work well, with 20% being allocated to speculative spending. Richard likens this to fishing in 2 lakes. The first is known to be brimming full of fish. The second is unknown and never fished before. The 20% budget may reveal some new and exciting potential, or it may not. But, if you don't dip your rod in you'll never know.

Parting Points

These parting remarks reinforce Richard's perspective on online marketing.

- Value your past experience – bringing a commercial positive approach to SEO and online marketing will give you a unique viewpoint to build your business
- Immerse yourself in the market and its language to improve your keyword selection
- Research the SEO market to learn new skills, techniques and keep up to date with developments in supporting software
- Remember: your client's success is your success

Richard Trussler
T: 01279 570075
richardtrussler@optimisemywebsite.co.uk
www.optimisemywebsite.co.uk
www.thesmallbusinessseocompany.co.uk

Selling Online via Mail Order

Spanishrings.com is an example of products sold online via mail order. Spanish Rings has its own domain name, independent hosting service, content management system and payment system with sales orders processed by PayPal.

Spanish Rings are Spanish-style flowerpot holders that provide the garden with an authentic Mediterranean feel. You may have walked along winding alleyways in Spain and seen flowers cascading down walls and balconies. Spanish Rings create the same effect.

Selling via mail order services online opens international opportunities. The UK is still the biggest market for Spanish Rings followed by the United States of America, then Australia and New Zealand. Garden products are acutely seasonal, with UK sales peaking from March to August – our Spring and Summer. However, as you're selling on the internet across the world, we receive orders from September to March when it is Spring and Summer in the Southern Hemisphere.

Online Marketing
www.spanishrings.com

International Mail Order

"Somewhere in the world it's Spring. Don't limit your business to one country - there's a whole world out there."

Key Advice

- Online marketing is a worldwide business. Your website is a global shop window. Think beyond borders
- Present your products well: provide sufficient information, use plain language, don't overcomplicate
- Make sure your website content is easy to navigate and easily understood
- Choose simple to operate and efficient shopping trolley software
- Always provide a phone contact to reassure customers that you're bona fide. Give them the option of ordering person-to-person by telephone
- Build confidence by operating an efficient and speedy delivery service

- Connect with your customers by adding feedback or photo gallery opportunities to involve them as much as possible
- Keep the product offering fresh with new ideas, product developments and promotions
- Incorporate a CMS (Content Management System) so you can make changes without having to pay a web developer to do it for you
- Explore ways to raise the profile of your company by attending trade and consumers shows and increase awareness through conventional and digital media
- Reassure customers with the latest anti-fraud software protection
- Don't over-invest before you start seeing the financial returns

Background

Spanish Rings create a Mediterranean style hanging garden. The simple but effective designs decorate walls, balconies, trellises and downpipes. Spanish Rings won the 1999 UK Garden Centre New Product of the Year at the prestigious Four Oaks Show.

In 2003, Water Rings water-storing flowerpot and hanging basket liners were launched to extend the range. Water Rings won the Silver Award in the 2004 UK National Gardening Awards. Both Spanish Rings and Water Rings have been featured on BBC's Ground Force and Garden Invaders programmes and on QVC - The Shopping Channel, in the Richard Jackson Gardening Show.

International Mail Order – a Lesson in Profit Margins

Spanish Rings were first launched as a garden centre product. The hope was to break into the big garden centre chains, department stores and DIY outlet. In fact it was the smaller independent garden centres that became our foothold in the market. When the BBC Ground Force programme was shown on television, the garden centre distribution rocketed from 25 to 75 garden centres in just 6 weeks. Spanish Rings were in the picture for just 8 seconds!

The turnover was respectable but the profit margin was severely reduced due to garden centres expecting:

- A 45% trade profit margin
- Free delivery
- Free display stands
- Credit for any returned stock
- To take up to 60 days to pay Spanish Rings invoices

Not surprisingly, the focus shifted to:

- Spring and Summer UK Flower Shows and cash sales direct to the public
- Supplying UK mail order catalogues ,for one-drop delivery and healthy margins
- QVC television sales
- Export sales to USA and Canada mail order companies and Australia, Sweden and Germany
- Direct UK mail order sales
- International mail order sales to private individuals

In case you're wondering why the wholesale route was not taken, the answer is that Spanish Rings was seen as a one product company and wholesalers usually favour companies with many brands or products to go into their catalogues.

The reason why Spanish Rings did not break into the big garden centre chains was that the big chains prefer to deal with wholesalers. Catch 22. The moral of this story is to focus on the most relevant routes to market that you have a chance to influence.

Parting Points

When planning a mail order business, whether within the UK or internationally these points could act as a useful checklist:

- Consider whether mail order is a stand-alone business engine or an adjunct to another sales route - for example, making products available online that you sell through other conventional channels
- Create a website that is fully functional, both in terms of the sales process, and for marketing support. This could involve email marketing, newsletters and SEO techniques, possibly involving Google Adwords and also incorporating links and back-links via article marketing
- Become familiar with available keyword software for words and phrases to help boost search engine rankings
- Build customer lists and prepare regular cycles of communication, to keep them aware of you and your products without being annoying or invasive
- Refresh your Home Page and graphics regularly. Google does like to see websites frequently updated, so add content to your site to increase awareness
- Remember to add social media links to your site, as sharing information and being generous with advice and guidance is welcomed by customers
- Use the website tactically with the changing seasons or events in the calendar to optimise sales opportunities

Steve Bridger
www.spanishrings.com

Working from Home – Adjusting to the Change

It's vital to keep overheads as low as possible, and cash flowing smoothly in the early stages of starting a business. Working from home could be a solution, especially where you venture out from your home to meet customers, whether developing an MLM proposition, representing a franchise or offering freelance services. For instance, a personal trainer may hire a venue to hold classes that are organised using the phone and computer back in the home office.

Working from home has both attractions and issues you need to consider. We're not talking about people who are employed or involved with flexible working. I'm talking about people who are using their home as a stopgap until business premises become available, or those who are starting completely afresh, perhaps as a result of redundancy, or just ready for a new beginning.

Let's skip over the obvious benefits of working from home, including, no more commuting, controlling your work schedule, being your own boss, working the hours that suit you. The flipside of these undoubted attractions is the need to adjust to being alone and working alone.

There's no more banter in the workplace, no people to talk to over a cup of coffee, just you and the whole unstructured day to shape to your will. This calls for personal discipline and, to some extent, re-booting your brain to the new reality. I confess that when I went freelance, it felt really strange going into town during the working day and being surrounded by young mums pushing prams and retired folk walking along as if the whole world had gone into slow motion. It did take some time to adjust.

You've got to make your own rules - where there are no rules.

While you don't have to replicate a normal 9am-5pm working day, you do need structure to earn a living. Inevitably, there are distractions: the kids arriving back from school, a big match on TV, a hot summer's day outside and so on. The aim is to strike a balance with a place to work that is a separate space from the rest of the family. Ground rules for interruptions and disturbances need to be understood. There's no need to beat yourself up if you transgress once in a while – you just have to make up the time in the evening or weekend to achieve the required result.

Make flexibility work for you. Accept the new reality and work effectively with you in control.

Legal and Tax Issues

You'll need to consider and get expert advice, on both the personal and the tax ramifications of running a business from your home. Personally, your status may either be self-employed or, if you've set up a limited company you could be seen as employed by the company. Either way, you'll be responsible for keeping records for Income Tax and National Insurance purposes. You must register as being self-employed with your local tax office.

From the business viewpoint, there may be an issue with regards to the payment of local council tax, depending on use. Linked to this is the possible payment of business rates (termed non-domestic rates). The rule of thumb is that if space in the house – a bedroom for example – is used for business purposes but is still used as bedroom, the council tax and property rates demand is unlikely to change.

On the other hand, if the main function of the premises changes then the building may be reclassified as being commercial premises. A decision is based on the extent and frequency of business use. If you decide to convert a garage into an office, the garage would be designated as change of use and liable to business rates. The adjoining house would remain on residential rates. Once again, speak to experts in the field, listen to and act on their advice.

For more information:
UK: www.businesslink.gov.uk
USA: www.yourhomebusinesses.com
Australia: www.workfromhomeaustralia.com

Working from Home vs. Home Working

To avoid any possible confusion, there is a difference between 'working from home' and 'home working'.

Working from home is using your private premises as a base to run your own business.

Home working is where you perform tasks, usually piecework (paid by the individual item or piece) where you assemble items within your own home for payment, for instance:

- Circuit boards – basic cutting/fixing
- Collage - basic cutting/sewing
- Envelope making - basic cutting/gluing
- Computer covers - basic cutting/gluing

With home working, you're paid a fixed fee per item from an employer, either directly or working through an agent. For more information about home working, log on to www.homeworking.com.

Popular Start-Up Options
4
High Street Retail

The siren call of the High Street can intoxicate. You may have dreamt of opening your own shop, creating your cherished vision with crowds of people beating a path to your door. It can happen. It does happen. That's why so many gamble, and why so many get drunk with the thought of success, only to be left with the mother of all hangovers.

It breaks my heart to see empty units burst into energetic life, as someone full of positivity and hope, has the shop fitters working to get ready for the first day of trading. Six months later, there's whitewash on the windows and the only sounds are hammers nailing up the 'To Let' board. We do not want this to be you.

Without doubt, the high street is a massive challenge for anyone, even in good times, but especially now in the teeth of a recession, with consumer demand falling off a cliff.

I've puzzled over the reasons for failure in either supplying a service (like running a restaurant) or selling goods at retail. Broadly speaking, they fall into two areas with failure as a toxic mixture of both.

One

The first set of reasons are to do with the high entry costs of either owning or leasing retail property – rent, rates, deposits, legal, insurance, shop fitting, utilities and any dead costs involved with setting up in readiness to trade. Dead costs are those unavoidable outlays that need to be covered and are instrumental in starting a business and absorbed but do not directly generate income.

Two

The second set is man-made. Primarily, these are people who fall victim to one or more of these factors, they sell:

- The wrong products
- In the wrong place
- At the wrong time
- At the wrong price
- With the wrong financial plan in place
- And sometimes, they are the wrong people for the business, as they do not possess the necessary inter-personal skills.

Here's a Start-Up Story from Tony Mingoia who has been running a restaurant in East Molesey for years.

Running a Restaurant

Tony and Giuseppe Mingoia
Palazzo Restaurant
A Passion for Italian Food

*"Quality and service, without those,
people will not come back."*

Key Advice

Don't do it! Don't open a restaurant, unless you:

- Are prepared to work harder than you've ever worked before
- Accept the restaurant will become your way of life
- Can live with uncertainty, stress and constant pressure
- Are flexible and willing to make improvements
- Have two brains, one for business and one devoted only to your customers

Background

The Palazzo has been open for eleven years. For an independent family restaurant, that's quite an achievement. Their success is built on unremitting hard work, a total passion in what they do, and never forgetting, it's the customer who is number one.

Tony, with his sons, Giuseppe and Vince, keep it personal. Unlike a restaurant chain with a limited menu selection and most dishes coming pre-prepared, the Palazzo offers more choice, with fresh dishes cooked to order and reasonably priced. Personal skill and dedication, rather than the ability to operate a microwave, is their special ingredient.

The Business Brain

Eleven years ago, there were 5 eating places in the Palazzo's stretch of the high street. Today, there are 15. How did they survive?

- By choosing a prime location – close to a car park and dead centre in the busiest section of the high street
- Being large enough to cater for guests – either single tables or party bookings at lunch and dinner

- Using a seated bar area for drinks, snacks and coffees, morning, noon and night
- Having pavement tables for when the weather is fine or as a smokers' retreat
- Offering readily affordable prices to encourage frequent visits
- Setting a weekly turnover target that recognises different weekday, weekend and seasonal patterns. You must calculate your weekly break-even figure to match turnover
- Welcoming private bookings for the restaurant
- Booking entertainers at the weekend
- Being consistent in quality
- Devising new menus and introducing dishes to cater for changing tastes, for instance including a good selection of vegetarian dishes
- Promoting special Christmas and New Year menus for private and corporate bookings
- Importantly, having a style of service that's attentive without being overbearing or intrusive - one that is sensitive to the mood of your guests

Parting Points

Tony sipped his espresso and pondered advice for someone thinking of opening a restaurant.

These were his parting pointers:

- Think carefully about your market. Is your concept right for the area and will it match the customers profile in your locality, at least enough to establish a solid and loyal customer base.
- Have a sufficient financial buffer to carry you through quiet periods. Creating customer loyalty takes time and it may be months before you break-even and cover fitting-out and initial running costs.

- Hire experienced staff. Better to have a few good people than amateurs who can damage your reputation. Be prepared to lend a hand to anything that needs doing. Keep it lean. Only have extra bodies on the floor when demand will pay for them.
- It's not unusual to experience frequent periods of low sales in the restaurant business, remember the bank can withdraw support at any time, and if you haven't got a good track record, you must assume they probably will.
- Don't underestimate the time it takes to meet all the different health and safety and environmental regulations involved in the catering business.
- As soon as you've created a regular, sustainable income, with a business model that has been tried and tested, look to gain the freehold of your chosen premises.

With the coffee cup now empty, Tony finished where he started with quality and service.

"Remember, you're not just selling food. If people make the choice to walk through your door, they want to absorb the atmosphere; relax and enjoy being with friends. For the time they're with you, they want put the outside world 'on-hold'. Our duty is to make that brief time special – every time."

The Palazzo Restaurant
T: 0208 979 5577
info@palazzorestaurant.co.uk
www.palazzomolesey.co.uk
98 Walton Road, East Molesey, Surrey KT8 0DL

Running a Sub-Post Office
Kanu Patel & Vishnu Desai

Kanu Patel
Molesey Sub-Post Office

"Don't go into a business – unless you know the business".

Key Advice

- Becoming a sub-postmaster is a responsible job in the community; don't underestimate the demands or overestimate the income
- Your customers are your livelihood. Treat them with respect and earn their respect in return
- Create a second-string income within your premises to work in harmony with the Post Office service.

Background

Kanu has been with the Post Office for over forty years; the last seventeen have been in East Molesey. The site of the current MSOP (Modified Sub-Post Office) was originally a bakers' in a prime position in a central parade of shops. For anyone considering becoming a sub-postmaster, there are a stringent set of requirements that need to be satisfied before the Post Office will approve the establishment of a new sub-post office. Principally, these involve its location and ability to

service enough customers to make it a going concern – and, of course, the necessity to make the premises secure.
You can view these in detail at:
http://www.nfsp.org.uk/Becoming_a_Subpostmaster.asp

The Responsibilities

Taking on the role of sub-postmaster demands dedication and commitment. You will be running a complex multi-faceted business and your customers will rely on you to provide a consistent and professional service. Businesswise, attention to detail is vital. Any shortages when cashing up at the end of the day must be made good by the sub-postmaster. All stockholding is logged on a central Post Office computer and auditors can visit at any time to check receipts and control systems.

This is a People Business

The Post Office performs a vital service to the community and as such, the aptitude and attitude of the sub- postmaster and his staff, (in this case) the invaluable Vishnu, are key factors in the smooth running of the office.

These are the personal characteristics that Kanu feels are essential:

- Full and up-to-date knowledge of Post Office services, gained through frequent training sessions
- Preparedness to work hard and provide a consistent level of service day in, day out
- Good communication and language skills, showing patience to customers who may not understand the details and requirements of Post Office services
- Showing particular consideration and help for the disabled, elderly or people who clearly need assistance
- Patience. Don't allow demanding customers to get to you

Second String

Over the last 20 years, over one third of UK Post Offices have closed. With changes in government policy and retailing habits, it is important to develop a second supporting string to supplement your Post Office business. In Kanu's case, this has been to stock a choice of stationery, sealing tape, boxes and envelopes, as well as a range of greetings cards. You're bound to see sub- post offices in newsagents and general grocery stores. The Post Office will attract customers who are likely to make additional purchases. It is these second string income streams that will increase commercial viability.

As you would expect, Valentine's Day, Mother's Day and Christmas are the high volume occasions in the year for letters, cards and parcels. However, with the increasing use email, the number of items sent by conventional mail is falling and as the Post Office pays commission on individual items of postage, it is essential that sub-postmaster must have entrepreneurial and business management skills to supplement the Post Office income.

Parting Points

Kanu and Vishnu work as a team. Before he joined the Post Office, Vishnu ran his own high street CTN (Confectionery, Tobacco and Newsagent) business and was well-versed in financial management. These are pointers they would like to pass on to people exploring the Post Office as a business opportunity.

- This is a pennies business. The commission on each sale is small but the volume potential is considerable. This is not a get-rich-quick business.
- 95% of customer visits result in a sale, so you must see each and every customer as making a small but important contribution to your income

- Search for a location that has a good mix of personal and business customers, and is close to other essential shops and services that people will visit on their way to your counter
- As the role of the sub-postmaster is a responsible one, you must act responsibly inside and outside of the office

Kanu Patel
Molesey Post Office
140 Walton Road, East Molesey, Surrey KT8 0HP

High Street – Priority Points

Location and Position – Two make or break factors

Location concerns whether your business is right for the locality, i.e. a particular area within a city, town or village.

Position is the site you've chosen within a high street, parade of shops or other selling location.

Ask yourself 3 things when you're considering where to base your business:

1. Is there sufficient demand for your product or service?

2. Does it fit with the income range and lifestyle of the community that you plan to enter? Would you open a tattoo parlour in an upmarket high street? Probably not.

3. Are there any businesses in competition with your ideas?

In our small urban village there are 7 hairdressers in the same stretch of road. That's slicing the onion very thinly. Are there enough heads to cut to sustain a good income for all 7 businesses? Probably not.

Position:

Let's assume that you've done your research and have good evidence that your business would thrive in a certain locality. How do you refine and fix your position within the high street?

Here are some suggestions:

*   Visit the high street a number of times at different times of the day, and on different days, to get a feeling for the dynamics, and the ebb and flow of customers

- Take note of the age and social mix. Is the mix a representative cross-section of the community or one with a particular bias that would suit your type of business

- Check the make-up of high street shops. Is there a balanced mix of retail shops, restaurants, a chemist, a post office and a supermarket, to attract a wide cross section of shoppers? Keep an eye on the number of charity shops. This may be a reflection of the economic buoyancy of the town or village. Many charity shops could indicate a less buoyant area as they do not have to generate the same trading returns as a commercial concern

- The car parking provision. What is their distance from the shops, parking prices and number of spaces available? What is the quality of the train, bus and road links to the surrounding area. How good are the services?

Footfall - Passing Trade Magnets and Windows

Factors affecting the position of premises:

1. Footfall - How many people directly pass your intended shop? Is it well positioned?

2. Passing trade – Apart from people actually walking by, is the shop in a good position to be seen by passing cars and buses and easy to stop and park by?

3. Magnets – Shopper magnets are places like a supermarket, a sub-post office and banks that attract people on a regular basis. Potential customers will be attracted by these magnets and drawn to your selling proposition.

4. Windows –Your shop is literally your window on the world. As such, it needs to be large enough to create a striking display, grab attention and encourage people to enter the shop. I know that last sentence is crushingly obvious and warrants a Homer Simpson "d'oh!" However, you'd be surprised at the number of shops that rarely, if ever, refresh their front windows.

Think of the road outside a shop as a flowing river, with shoals of lovely 'shopper-fish', swimming up and down 24 hours a day, 7 days a week. By refreshing your window display to suit new fashion trends, the changing seasons, show new stock and at Christmas time, you'll keep potential customers interested and intrigued. If they don't buy themselves they may recommend your shop to friends and family. Inside a shop, you will need to mirror the window display with regular rotation of stock. Make sure you have a range of prices to suit every pocket. Even a small sale contributes to cash flow.

Premises Particulars

We've looked at some of the key outside issues of location and position. Now I'd like to focus on the inside of the premises and look at leases and responsibilities for the upkeep of the premises. Here are some tips:

1. Retail Classifications

Retail premises in the UK fall into four different categories of use. These classifications determine what type business functions can be carried out within the premises. In the High Street, retail premises fall into Class A and are divided in A1, A2 or A3. An estate agent must state what classification the property falls into.

Here's a classification breakdown for high street premises:

Class A1. Shops

Use for all or any of the following purposes:
(a) The retail sale of goods other than hot food,
(b) As a Post Office,
(c) The sale of tickets or as a travel agency,
(d) The sale of sandwiches or other cold food for consumption off the premises,
(e) Hairdressing,
(f) The direction of funerals,
(g) The display of goods for sale,
(h) The hiring out of domestic or personal goods or articles,
(i) The reception of goods to be washed, cleaned or repaired, where the sale or service is to visiting members of the public.

Class A2. Financial and Professional Services

Use for the provision of:
(a) Financial services
(b) Professional services - other than health or medical services
(c) Any other services (including use as a betting office) which it is appropriate to provide in a shopping area where the services are provided principally to visiting members of the public.

Class A3. Food and Drink

Use for the sale of food or drink for consumption on the premises or of hot food for consumption off the premises.

You must adhere to the stated use of the classification. It is possible to apply for a 'Change of Use' from the local authority but this will be the subject of a special application.

If you intend to use high street premises as an office, it will fall into the 'B' classification.

Class B1. Business

For use as an office, other than a use within class A2 (financial and professional services).

Licences and Permits

You may need special licences or permits from the local authority to perform a business function. You will need a premises licence to sell alcohol or a special permit to use the space in front of your shop to sell goods. If you're opening a taxi or minicab service, or if there's gambling on the premises, a bookmaker's for example, you will need a licence.

Check with your local authority on licences or permits if you are planning to operate a:

- massage parlour, tattooing and body-piercing, acupuncture, electrolysis or skin-colouring establishment
- market or become a street trader
- sex shop
- pet shop
- boarding kennels

2. Leasing and Renting Premises

This is a subject that warrants an entire book. My task is to attempt a digestible overview so you have enough information to consider the issues involved before you meet an estate agent and brief your legal representative.

Don't sign on the dotted line with an estate agent or landlord until you take legal advice. Do not rush into an agreement, only to realise that your chosen premises are a disaster that'll make a gigantic hole in your bank account.

If you do decide to go ahead, it would be advisable to include a break clause to release you from the agreement after a certain period of time, and be able to leave the premises without penalty, if your business for whatever reason encounters problems and cannot continue trading.

Definitions

The landlord is the owner of the property or the person or organisation owning an existing lease of the property.

The tenant is the occupier of the property or the person paying rent to a landlord.

The heads of terms is a summary of the agreement between the landlord and tenant. It is the document used to instruct lawyers to produce the formal lease.

Landlord Leases

The usual process is for estate agents to be your first port of call. They will show you round a number of potential properties. This will give you an opportunity to gauge the position, price, size and general condition of the range of properties on the market.

Bear in mind that you may need to gain the approval of the landlord for any initial shop fitting work, signage and any changes to the basic layout of the premises.

Any work undertaken will have to comply with building regulations plus health and safety and satisfy access laws for the disabled. This could involve installing a wheelchair ramp.

Once you've taken possession, you will be responsible for maintenance and general upkeep of the premises.

Some basic elements of a Lease

You should expect a landlord to have a lease prepared for you to consider. These are some of the areas you may see and discuss with your legal advisor. A lease will generally include these provisions:

- The identity of the parties – who is the landlord and who is the tenant.
- The rent, any rent review and rent deposit figure
- The nature of any guarantees required
- The length of the rental term and tenancy renewal rights
- Any break rights to break the lease early
- Whether a tenant will be offered a new lease when the original lease comes to an end
- The rights to assign, sublet or share the premises
- The maintenance, repair and alteration obligations
- Which party is responsible for payment of insurance costs
- The VAT status of the premises
- The right of access to the property
- The right of the landlord to 'forfeit' – that is to cancel the lease, if the tenant fails to pay the rent or observe its obligations under the lease.

Additionally, a landlord may volunteer if any alternative or special lease terms are available, or whether the rental figure would vary if any lease terms are modified. For example, a landlord may reduce the rental figure if a tenant pays for improvements to the property that will be of considerable future value and benefit to the landlord as owner.

Break Clauses

A break clause gives a tenant a right to terminate a lease during the lease term. These occasions will be agreed and could be on a rolling basis that allows the tenant to break the agreement at any time after a certain date has passed. The tenant will be required to give notice of its intention to exercise the break.

It is very important to check only any pre-conditions that must be met by the tenant, including keeping up to date with rent payments and giving vacant possession of the premises. It is advisable for a solicitor to advise on these matters.

High Street Start-Up Stories

This is an excellent time to introduce Matt and Tamsin Court. Tamsin and Matt took a step-by-step approach to starting and developing their own antiques and gifts business. They gained experience of different premises, landlords and leases before they opted to buy freehold.

Turn the page to meet them.

Matt & Tamsin Court
Belle Epoque
Antiques for Modern Living

"We are not gamblers. We were determined to make a go of it with our own money, without a bank loan."

Key Advice

- Adopt a rolling growth mind-set – don't overstretch yourself and take it one step at a time
- Fund growth from your own resources – avoid loans and avoid debt
- Be flexible in your approach – don't persist with something that's not working
- Research the market, keep it fresh, and offer price points for every pocket
- Don't try to do everything yourself
- Make time for friends and family

Background

Matt was working in IT up in town. Tamsin was a secondary school teacher. They both wanted to work together, do something that they loved and attempt to have some control over their own destinies. Tamsin's stepdad had years of experience in the 'trade' side of antiques, mainly selling dark wood and traditional items of furniture to dealers and attending trade-only shows up and down the country.

Ten years ago Tamsin and Matt made their first move by renting a space at Palace Antiques, an indoor antiques market divided into small rented booths. They held down their day jobs and funded expenses out of monthly pay packets. This research in action gave them the experience and confidence to move on and move up.

Getting Serious

Couples working together need symmetry. There are always bound to be differences of opinion, but for something to work smoothly over a period of time, both parties need to play a mutually supportive role. In Belle Epoque Tamsin performs the role of sourcing, buying and presentation. Matt uses his IT skills for business and financial management, while devoting his woodworking talents to giving a little 'TLC' to shop window stock.

In 2005, a lock-up shop became available in the heart of the village. Matt and Tamsin took the decision to sell their house, downsize and free up finance to pay the rent, rates and buy opening stock. Belle Epoque became their day job. At this point, the greater percentage of stock was in medium to large items of furniture, many pieces being sourced from France.

It soon became clear that, due to rising prices and even steeper rises in the exchange rate, the margins on French sourced stock were being cut drastically. This prompted a review of sales strategy, as a new approach was needed, an approach that crystallised the basic selling proposition of Belle Epoque.

Antiques for Modern Living

Knowing your market is good advice for any would-be business. In Belle Epoque's case, it shaped their future strategy. Molesey grew rapidly in the late Victorian period from 1835 to 1890. The village has a high percentage of Victorian and Edwardian properties, and more recent 'quality' residences. Tamsin and Matt focused on people who wanted to keep the essential character, but give their homes a refreshing modern look.

This called for the introduction of attractive antique pieces as decoration, a range of stylish gift items and some physically smaller and less expensive furniture pieces. The result is a full range of choice, either for the home or as simple gift purchases. Importantly, the new stock strategy means that there is a price point for practically every customer.

2009 and Beyond

2009 was massively important. After four years, Tamsin and Matt changed status from tenants to freeholders by buying a new shop at number 88 Walton Road. The new sales strategy is working and word has spread, with customers now visiting the shop from further afield.

Parting Points:

As you would expect, the new shop needed a full refit and these pointers would be useful to anyone thinking of opening a high street retail unit:

- Don't wait until everything is perfect. A closed shop is a closed till – start earning as soon as you can.
- Try not to take any forced delay personally – manage the process and build in contingency funding to give you some flexibility and lessen any stress.
- Regularly refresh your window with new items to attract attention. Design the window with different themes or changing seasons to catch the eye.

Belle Epoque
T: 0208 941 9269
enquires@belleepoque.me.uk
www.belleepoque.me.uk
88 Walton Road, East Molesey, Surrey KT8 0DL

High Street Retail
Bicycle Shop

Neil Brand
Neil's Wheels
Bikes, Spares and Repairs

"You've got to want it with your whole being. You need to ride the knock-backs to get you there."

Key Advice

- Become an expert in your chosen field
- Gain experience by getting paid to work in your chosen field before setting up on your own
- Learn from others' mistakes
- Take time to develop your own special vision – what will make you different?
- Develop your business skills, especially in money management
- Come back stronger from setbacks
- Know your market
- Treat every customer as if they are your only customer

Background

At school, Neil got the chance of a week's work experience at the Raleigh bike shop in Surbiton. He did the menial stuff nobody wanted to do, but also watched the engineers strip down and rebuild bikes in need of a repair or service. Something clicked. He was offered a Saturday job that morphed into full-time and pretty soon it was Neil who was doing the repairs and servicing.

When Raleigh decided to close its service centres, he went to work in a series of cycle shops, mainly concentrating on repairs and servicing, but also learning management skills including customer sales, general administration and stock control. This was extremely valuable on-the-job training that would prove indispensible in the future.

Don't get the idea this period was all plain sailing. Neil worked at a cycle shop in Walton that changed hands and he was out of a job. He then moved to Kingston for 3 years before that shop closed due to poor management. In 2006, he was made redundant yet again. This time, when offered the option of a financial pay-out or a choice of quality tools and workshop equipment, he opted for the tools. These are the same tools he's still using now, probably at the same time you're reading this.

Two Steps Forward One Step Back

In October 2006, Neil put the finishing touches to his first business plan. He applied and won a business grant of £4,000. Just as he was about to receive the money he received another knock-back – the grant was slashed to £1,500 and his plans fell apart, including advanced negotiations for a shop. He went back to work, his dream on hold.

Good Out of Evil

To make matters worse, another cycle shop opened a shop in Bridge Road at the other end of the village. The prospect of two cycle shops in competition would have been disastrous.

Fate lent a hand. The shop closed within six months. Their misfortune and mismanagement proved a salutary business lesson. Neil observed that:

- They'd misjudged the market, selling only very expensive new bikes
- They charged higher prices for identical bikes sold by an established cycle shop in nearby Kingston upon Thames
- The shop was in a narrow one-way street, with no displays allowed on the pavement
- No parking nearby meant little passing trade
- Poor customer service by people who knew little about bikes.

Neil's Wheels Finally Arrives – June 2010

Fourteen years after his week-long work experience, Neil Brand finally opened his shop.

This is his concept, now a reality offering:

- A shop selling both new and second-hand bicycles. The pre-owned bikes being repaired and renewed at extremely reasonable prices
- A wide selection, from children's cycles to racing and road bikes
- Attentive, friendly, expert service by Neil, Petor, and Maxi-Bon
- Opening hours to suit his customers
- A great position in the high street, with bikes on the pavement to catch the eye of passers- by

- No competition – other shops are selling new bikes without repairs and service on-site

Parting Points

With his hands stained with WD40, and a smile on his face, these were Neil's tips to someone thinking of setting up their own business:

- Don't give up
- Believe in yourself and what you're doing
- Take advice and stay positive
- Don't blow you money on something that's not properly grounded and thought through
- Watch your cash flow like a hawk

Neil's Wheels
T: 0208 979 0707
60 Walton Road, East Molesey, Surrey, KT8 0DL

High Street Retail
Music Shop

Trevor Marshall
Musicland East

"People buy people. We don't pressure. A personal, friendly service is a must for a small business. Positive word-of-mouth is everything - it keeps people coming back."

Key Advice

- Create an original point of difference
- Choose your location with care, don't just go for the lowest rent and rates
- Do your homework on the market – avoid competition if at all possible
- Don't take a line of credit you can't meet - ideally don't take one at all!
- Don't over-commit yourself stock- wise – make sure you can turn it over
- Offer a variety of goods at a range of prices to turn a coin

- Give an expert personal service to gain sales and attract repeat business
- Remember that positive word-of-mouth is priceless

Background

In the early 80s, Trevor was a music teacher in Canada. He was also gigging five or six nights a week with his band. This kept him happy, busy and generated a decent income. His teaching activities were on a franchise basis, in association with the Canadian Conservatory of Music. During the daytime, he hired small venues within a 25-mile radius of his home and charged students for guitar lessons.

His lessons grew in popularity, to a point where he needed more space, but didn't want to pay the hugely increased fee venues were demanding. That's when life gave him a helping hand: a friend hearing of his dilemma suggested the use of an empty shop for $125 a month.

And so it started with guitar lessons in an empty shop.

Trevor invested a modest sum in some basic stock – acoustic guitars, strings, plectrums, and teaching books. It didn't take long before the shop became a focal point. His teaching sessions started and finished when he wanted. This was normally in the evening, after the kids were back from school and adults could turn up for lessons after work. Trevor knew instinctively to put his customers first and play to their rhythm, rather than lay down his own strict tempo of opening and closing hours.

The empty shop became a music shop that gave music lessons, two solid income streams in one – inspired!

Fast Forward to Molesey -1997

Trevor missed the buzz of Britain. While back on holiday from Canada, for interest more than anything else, he looked at music shops in Weybridge, Walton, Cobham and Esher. He saw that they were all one-idea-outfits. Not long afterwards, the freehold of numbers 52-54 Walton Road for the shop and the apartment above passed to Mr Marshall. Musicland East opened its doors, selling guitars, banjos, violins, recorders, drums, keyboards, mics and amps from £40 to £600. Lessons start at 3.30pm and finish at 8pm – six days a week.

Fourteen years later, the business has built a loyal clientele. As the shop is staffed with musicians, there's a laid-back, relaxed and friendly atmosphere. Musicland East has become part of the community, with students from seven to seventy taking grades for ACM exams (Academy of Contemporary Music) or for their own enjoyment.

Location, Location – You've Got to Get a Good Location

Trevor credits the location of Musicland East as a key factor in his success. If you've no passing trade, if you're in an isolated backwater, sometimes even if you're on the wrong side of the road, your location can make or break you. Don't let your desire to get going blind you to blatantly obvious drawbacks. If a landlord is offering cheaper rates then ask yourself why? Wherever you choose make sure there's a tenants break clause in the rental agreement.

The location of Musicland East has these benefits:

1. A large wrap-round corner window and straight high street window clearly visible to traffic without any blockage to passers' line-of-sight.
2. Situated on the high street, but with access on a side road, so that customers – particularly parents and

children attending lessons, can safely park and walk to the shop.

3. A large car park nearby for customers to plan a shopping trip while visiting Musicland East.

Parting Points

When asked what advice he would give to someone thinking of starting a business, he sipped his coffee, thought for a moment and replied:

- Be prepared to shoulder the responsibility and workload yourself, but don't be afraid to ask for help.
- It's not the size of the business, or how many branches you have, or how big a turnover, it's how much money 'sticks' to your fingers. It's the bottom line that counts. Good luck!

Trevor Marshall
0208 979 9443
52-54 Walton Road, East Molesey, Surrey KT8 0DL

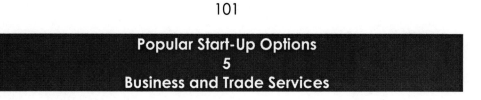

Popular Start-Up Options
5
Business and Trade Services

Working on Your Own

Frequently, professional or trade services are provided by one person working alone, selling their skills and talents. It takes a great deal of conviction, confidence and ability to go into business. Working from home, without the support of fellow colleagues, and without support systems provided by an employer can be a scary experience.

Don't be put off. The experience is liberating.

You just need time to adjust to the new reality and adapt your working life accordingly. You'll no longer be a hamster spinning round in a corporate wheel.

Most importantly, working alone does not have to be lonely.

For example, as a marketing communications freelance writer, I'm always out seeing clients in their offices, having meetings in coffee shops or shooting off to networking sessions. I welcome the peace and quiet of returning home, powering up the computer, listening to music, and starting to type without interruption. The advantage of being able to organise my schedule to suit my workload priorities is an effective way of managing time.

9 to 5 is over. You'll be working 7 days a week if you need to, less if you don't. You'll work solidly for hours or work smartly in less time to get things done. Why? Because the only thing that really matters to someone working on their own is the quality of work they produce and the amount of money they need to generate to meet your financial and personal goals.

Are you a Lark or an Owl?

When's the best time for you to produce your best quality work?

Do you leap up in the morning, full of energy and ready to face the challenges of the day, or do you mentally start the day after lunch?

A lark fizzes with energy in the morning. So, organise your workload and focus your brain power then, when you're fresh and creative. Leave the afternoon for research, planning and administration, when your mind starts to flag.

Turn this suggestion on its head if you're an owl.

Do the undemanding jobs in the morning. Work positively when you feel the zip and zing of inspiration later in the day. Plan your workload accordingly. Identifying what kind of person you are, either Lark or Owl, will allow you to direct your energies at the optimum time to best effect.

Set the working day to the natural rhythm of your body and brain.

Luigi Chiodaroli and Hilton Taylor
Elite Computing Solutions
Total IT Solutions for Small Businesses and Home Users

"Do a job that's always going to push you. Do something you love."

Key Advice

- If a one-man-band, be proud and confident of your talent
- Don't undersell or undervalue yourself – you're delivering a personal service that will often out-perform competitors with your skill and dedication
- Be disciplined in your work ethic – be totally committed
- Keep up to date with invoicing and chase money due to you
- Provide an exceptional service. Be prepared to go the extra mile for valued clients
- Build strong business and personal relationships

- Always strive to widen and strengthen your business base – don't rely on a few clients. Spread the risk.

Luigi

Luigi was brought up in South Africa. Life was a struggle, with rewards earned from a willingness to be more committed than the next man. His father, Giovanni, a self-made man, was an inspirational role model, who greatly influenced Luigi's work ethic. By the age of 21, Luigi had built up a small building company, and then progressed to something completely different. He became a runner on a film set, working his way up to be Grip and then Best Boy. These are technical people who are involved with the production process in the studio or on location.

The year was 1998. Jackie Chan's 'Who am I?' film was being shot on location. The experience would change his life, for two reasons: one for the lessons he learned from Jackie Chan the other, literally, by accident. Even though Jackie was a massively successful film star, he made time for every member of the crew. When the filming was nearing completion, Jackie gave the crew a memento of an embroidered T shirt - everyone except Luigi. Seeing this oversight, within 24 hours, Jackie arranged for one more XL shirt to be embroidered and flown out from Hong Kong. This was a life lesson in professional excellence and personal motivational skills that Luigi would never forget.

Break a Leg

The theatrical saying for 'good luck' is 'break a leg'. Luigi did exactly that. Six weeks in plaster reading magazines on IT that led to a totally new career path. He embarked on a 12-week working holiday to England and stayed. Over the next 9 years, he moved from learning basic networking and cabling techniques to becoming a technical director.

Going Solo

In 2007, Luigi went solo. He had one client and operated from a bedroom that doubled as a workshop, with a maintenance bench built into the corner. He placed adverts in local magazines, put flyers through letterboxes and joined a business networking group. A year later, Luigi had left the bedroom for a fully kitted-out workplace and more work than one man could handle.

Hilton

As the business grew, Luigi wanted someone to join him with high-level experience to complement his skills and help drive the business forward. Hilton is not your average IT professional. His background is with large corporates. He was used to operating management structures and procedures. Hilton's technical skills, coupled with his commercial background, made him the perfect candidate.

Hilton relished the challenge of helping Elite become even more successful. The CRM (customer relationship management) and back-office systems have made a significant contribution to a business that is frequently an emergency service to clients in a crisis. When a problem has to be resolved quickly, it's important to manage costs and invoice accordingly.

Mutual respect is the cornerstone of Luigi's and Hilton's relationship, mutual respect for each other as individuals, and for their respective IT talents. They appreciate that they're running a high pressure business and that they each need their own space from time to time to unwind after a stressful job. The fact that they had a friendship before they became business partners also helps to diffuse any tension. It's a rule that any issues are aired and resolved without being allowed to rankle.

This piece is being written in 2011 - the beginning of the third year since Luigi and Hilton joined forces and four years since Luigi started knocking on doors. Working together, they've almost tripled the Elite client base while still delivering the same high quality of service.

Time Management Tip – Selling Time

If you provide a service to clients, it all comes down to managing time effectively. This simple guideline used by Hilton and Luigi, will help you direct your efforts to generate the returns you'll need:

- First, calculate what you NEED to make each week or month - the amount you'll need to cover all your overheads, expenses and a living wage.
- Second, calculate what you WANT to make to create a financial buffer or support any personal requirements.
- Divide your hourly rate into both of the above, to reveal how many billable hours you need to work to achieve your aims.
- In IT, your main source of income is time and expertise, not the margin you make on buying and selling components.

Parting Points

Here are a couple of final thoughts on IT specifically and generally on providing a service.

- Spend time building confidence and trust – try to relate to your clients on a professional and personal level.
- Expect a high level of stress and emotion – to a client a computer crash feels like the end of the world.
- Be prepared to work unsociable hours. In IT, you're an emergency service forever on-call in a crisis.

- Try to manage demands as best you can. You could find yourself working all hours to the detriment of family relationships.
- As you're likely to be working at a fast pace, make time for invoicing a job. Don't neglect the money side as you rush out to rescue another IT crisis.

Elite Computing Solutions Ltd
T: 0203 137 5305
info@elitecs.co.uk
www.elitecs.co.uk

Business Services
Freelance Copywriter

Keith Grover

"Identify a niche in a growing market segment. Then develop your expertise within that area."

Key Advice

- Prepare a varied portfolio to promote your talents. Show different writing styles, textual content, client list and creativity

- If you have only a few examples, volunteer to do work for low cost or even for free to increase the size of your portfolio
- Avoid non-productive overheads - that's premises, staff and stock. Work from home or at a client's premises
- Develop a reputation for skilful writing within your chosen genre: descriptive, technical, expository, narrative, persuasive
- Explore free sources of business information on the internet
- Attend business networking events. You'll gain valuable free advice
- Ask to shadow and learn from someone who is already working in a capacity that is relevant to you
- Freelancing, by its very nature, is an on-off experience. Think about creating a second-string for extra income between projects

Background

Keith went into teaching after leaving Exeter University. He spent four years at a Bristol comprehensive school, teaching English to A Level. Still in his early twenties, he wanted a change of scene and applied to an English language school in Athens. As lessons started at 5pm and finished at 9pm, with the rest of the day free, it was a dream job – perhaps the best in the world.

Living and working in paradise brought Keith into contact with holiday tour reps working for the big UK operators. Being the kind of person who is always open to luck, he was offered a job in Athens meeting groups of tourists at the airport, escorting them down to Piraeus port and onto the ferries to the outlying islands. Keith was expected to socialise in the bars and taverns, walk along the sandy beaches with crystal clear azure water lapping the shoreline, and sip ouzo watching the sun slowly dip and disappear into the Aegean. No, this *was* the best job in the world.

The Right Words

Keith's talent as a writer proved to be a perfect match with his tour rep experience. SunMed Holidays was a specialist tour operator, focusing on the Greek islands. Having been a rep for them, Keith returned to the UK to work in their head office, and contract accommodation in Greece. He became the SunMed brochure manager responsible for pulling together the facts and figures on resorts, accommodation and creating a picture library. It was a natural progression for Keith to craft the right words for the brochure too, as he knew many of the people and places personally.

Keith devoted more and more of his time to copywriting. After leaving SunMed, he worked on the Habitat and The Pier brochures, and became aware of direct marketing. Direct marketing is the skill of making personal contact with individuals, or group of consumers within a particular target market. As you are speaking *directly* to them, commonly using letters, brochures and leaflets, the writing must be persuasive, informative and compelling - attributes that suited Keith down to the ground.

The Freelance Challenge

Direct Marketing was to be Keith's niche. His background as an English teacher gave him fluency in spelling and grammar. His experience in the travel industry created a strong portfolio that complemented his analytical and technical abilities. His understanding of marketing techniques rounded off an impressive set of skills. Yet, like all of us, he had to start somewhere to gain clients and generate an income.

He began by researching the market and contacting the Direct Marketing Association. He then drew up a list of direct marketing agencies and sent out letters of introduction and requests for a meeting. Out of 10 letters he would get 2 responses with invitations to "come and see us". Keith kept up to date with developments in the DM field reading weekly marketing magazines and making notes on which agencies were in the process of pitching for clients. The direct marketing sector grew rapidly, as did the demand for Keith's expertise. As a natural progression, Keith now finds he spends most of his time writing copy for websites and email marketing.

Parting Points

These last pieces of advice will help your preparation as a freelancer – whether it's as a marketing writer, journalist, photographer, graphic designer or any skilled position where projects are temporary in nature.

- In support of your portfolio, provide hard evidence of the results that your work produced.
- Prepare your own T and Cs. It's useful to have your own terms of business clear in your own mind and available in hard copy for a prospective client.
- Clarify the parameters of any brief – be clear about exactly what you're expected to do and by when
- Linked to the point above, agree your fees and payment procedure. Be alert to brief-creep, this is where a client asks you to do more as an assignment progresses - but expects to pay no more than the original fee.
- Communicate with a client regularly and prepare a summary of the brief to be signed-off, so all parties are in agreement with the task ahead.
- Beware of the goal posts being moved, don't take the word of junior clients as gospel – try to get confirmation of more senior managers if you tactfully can.
- Develop another income stream to complement your freelance work.
- Always maintain contact with past clients, while continually searching for new opportunities. Don't put all your eggs in one basket.

- Keep up to date with market trends and new business strands. Continually educate yourself to deliver a higher quality of service to your clients.
- Gather testimonials and put them on your website. If you haven't got a website, get one.
- Raise awareness of your business identity through business networking using social media, e.g. Twitter, ecademy, Linkedin.

Keith Grover
T: 01932 845 814
keith@freelancecopy.co.uk
www.freelancecopy.co.uk
www.networkinginsurrey.co.uk

Building your Freelance or Business Services Consultancy

Here's some advice gleaned from years of experience:

- First, to help you get started and become operational
- Secondly, to strengthen and develop your business base

To begin, you will need to:

1. Create Your Professional Identity, comprising:

- Your business, trading name and a new logo
- Business cards, designed and printed (see below for more information on business cards)
- A website. This can be a simple site, with your own domain name
- Email address, linked to the domain name – ideally not Yahoo or BT or hotmail.co.uk or Hotmail.com, as this looks like a personal rather than a business site
- Stationery – A4 letterheads and compliment slips

2. How to Build Your Business Lists

- Re-connect with past business clients
- Draw up a list of people/companies you would like to work with
- Check local or internet directories for potential new clients and confirm contact name, position and responsibility
- Join local business networking organisations to meet other small businesses and get free advice from people experienced in business start-ups
- Explore joining your local Chamber of Commerce for networking and assistance
- Start your own personal marketing programme by signing up to social media websites
- Search for local and international business networking opportunities.
- Pay commission for introductions and referrals to reward people who've put business your way. If financial payment is not appropriate, see whether a contra deal is acceptable. A contra arrangement is where an exchange of values takes place, but no money changes hands.

3. Develop your Portfolio of Work Experience

- Within your particular area of expertise, look for topics or aspects on which you can become an authority. For instance, if you're an expert in the general field of marketing communications learn all about the impact of social media so you can give guidance on this particular aspect.
Here's an example: If you're a landscape gardener, develop a reputation for patio decking. The idea is that you can increase the chance of your skills being used to meet different customer demands.
- As you progress, gather evidence of your work to impress future customers. Take before and after photos

of a job, showing the amazing results you've achieved. The same idea applies for builders, decorators, gardeners and all trade skills - take photos to show evidence of your work.

- The process of gathering evidence of your expertise is reinforced with genuine testimonials. I say genuine, because people can be cynical and believe that you've made them all up yourself. To avoid this, try to use the actual words of the person giving you the testimonial, type them in italics with speech marks and provide details of what job or service was provided and when it was done. If they agree, take a photo of the customer or even better, a short video.

4. Prepare your Terms and Conditions

- As with any business, you should prepare a list of your own T and Cs. Whether you're working freelance or as a sole trader, you need to have to hand a clear statement of your terms of business to refer to when first being engaged to work for a customer.
- Terms and conditions are there to protect your rights, limit your liabilities and provide you with some security.
- Due to the nature of their activities, many freelancers and sole traders conduct their businesses with informal verbal agreements. 9 times out of 10 this works smoothly. It is when disputes arise over issues such as quality, price, or time delays. Relations can become inflamed. In these circumstances, having given a customer your terms and conditions at the outset will help to resolve the situation. However, you must make a client aware of, and gain their agreement to, your terms of payment *before* work commences. Discuss and agree these issues in advance of any money changing hands.

Terms and Conditions may include:

- Your costs if you've given a fixed quote, otherwise include them in a separate cost estimate
- Delivery or commencement date of work
- Payment method by cash, cheque, online payment
- Timing of payment, amount of deposit or level of part-payment in advance
- Credit period, payment period after invoicing (In the UK there is a default 30 day settlement period)
- The right to charge interest on late payments
- An assurance of quality and competence
- Compliance with data protection regulations
- Dispute process and compensation claims

Please take advice from a lawyer to help draw up your business terms and conditions

5. Brief Creep – Letters of Confirmation

Brief Creep happens when a customer requests further services or tasks to be undertaken without any adjustment in payment terms. Whether deliberate or an oversight, this can cause problems for the freelancer or sole trader providing goods or a service.

The way to minimise this is to include a covering letter along with the original cost estimate. The covering letter will set down in detail what services or goods have been taken into consideration to prepare costings. In order that any extra expense, incurred later, can be identified.

Brief Creep is a common problem and affects a wide range of trade or professional services. Freelance creative services often encounter clients who continually make subjective changes to designs or written text. Builders get this all the time, when customers ask for extras and get annoyed when the bill arrives. The answer is to be open and explain the basis for any quote and, be sure to update the customer and get their agreement to proceed before any further expenses are incurred.

Business Services
Chrysalis – Family Wellbeing Consultancy

Karen Henfrey

"Love what you do. You've got to have passion – your business becomes your life."

Key Advice

- Everything takes time to grow. Have patience
- Look after yourself, emotionally, physically and spiritually
- When starting a business, the strain can be great. Value your network of friends and family as their support will be a great help in times of stress
- Be creative in your thinking. Believe in your judgement, but don't be afraid to ask for advice or help. Be receptive to new ideas
- If involved in a business partnership, clearly define the roles by creating mini-job descriptions, to clarify expectations and the level of commitment needed

- Build in time when dealing with big organisations, as obstacles and processes may take much longer than you think
- Have fun and schedule time in your diary to self-nurture yourself, by taking a walk or doing some exercise to get away from the work place. It will help to clear your mind, de-stress and think.

Background

Karen has been involved with caring for the young, those with special needs, and the physically handicapped, since she was fourteen years old. She was a volunteer with Playbus, a MSC (Manpower Services Commission) initiative, where a mobile play centre was driven to deprived areas for the enjoyment of children and to give their parents a brief respite. After college, Karen passed her NNEB exams (National Nursery Examination Board) and later qualified in sensory integrated studies for early years, visually impaired and the deaf.

Focus on the Family

Karen finessed her skills with years of practical application, including becoming a member of the Surrey Early Years Inspectorate. In 1997, she retrained to focus on the family as a Family Learning Co-ordinator. Nine years later, after yet another NHS shake-up, and another round of local authority cutbacks, Karen was made redundant and formed Chrysalis Parenting Consultancy with an ex-NHS colleague.

The concept was to offer a dedicated advice service to the family, from pre-natal to grandparent. The aim was to coach each individual to improve relationships and increase harmony within the family unit.

Chrysalis has developed programmes:

- For couples before they become parents

- To help new parents with their new arrival(s)
- On how to handle toddler tantrums
- To help young children overcome shyness, make friends and overcome bad habits
- To decode teenage angst and help to understand the biological confusion of youth
- To air and share parental issues with groups of parents
- To encourage relationship problem solving during special father and family days
- To put the fun back into family life and encourage young families to make positive changes
- To help calm young children in the Relax Kids Chill-out programme

Parting Points

This is Karen's advice if you're thinking of going into the field of consultancy, either alone or in partnership:

- Avoid debt – Chrysalis was funded by taking second jobs to cover launch and early running expenses
- Outsource bookkeeping and other business requirements, for example marketing and promotion, to support agencies. Concentrate on your own expertise
- Value your skills and keep them up to date
- Realise that you're never off-duty. Be prepared to promote yourself and your business. Always carry business cards and leaflets if you have them
- Attend business networking events – you may not win business directly, but you may meet people who'll help you succeed
- If in a partnership, prepare a practical working agreement and accept that people change if circumstances (private or business) change
- Get feedback from clients, learn from criticism, accept and enjoy praise
- Be organised in your back-office systems, especially for tax and accounting

- Fill in your year planner with key dates
- Keep office space separate from family space if you're working from home
- Sound upbeat, even if you're having a bad day
- Ensure you develop an exit strategy from the business

Karen Henfrey
M: 07790 252 936
karen@chrysalisparenting.co.uk
www.chrysalisparenting .co.uk

Business Services
Ergonomic & Healing Therapist

Maria Morris
Applied Ergonomics – Cold Light Laser – FLP Consultant

"Belief is a powerful business force. If you believe you'll be successful – you will be."

Key Advice

- You must really connect with what you want to do. You cannot divorce the commercial motivation from your personal instincts
- If what you're doing in business does not make your heart sing, don't do it
- Building a good business and personal reputation is everything. It takes time to create, but takes seconds to tarnish
- Don't self-limit your future ambitions as a reaction to previous setbacks and perceived failures in business or your personal life. Learn from partial successes and embrace the positive
- Move forward. Don't look back
- Don't become a working machine. Get your life in balance, remember the slogan, work, rest and play
- Take time away from the business to recharge
- If you're working alone: make sure you put a lone working policy in place to keep colleagues, friends and family in touch with your movements, especially if you're a woman working alone.

Background

Having read those bullet points, it'll come as no surprise that Maria has a health background in the NHS. Before she joined the commercial world, Maria was a senior occupational therapist assisting in the management of an outpatient department. She completed additional training to concentrate on vocational rehabilitation and became an expert in the field of ergonomics. Ergonomics is the study of the relationship between the human body and man-made working tasks. This could involve the design of workplace equipment to create a more harmonious and healthy working environment for individuals.

The Healing Touch

Following a further training period in the United States, and lecturing engagements in universities in the UK, Maria increased her activities in vocational rehabilitation in return to work programmes and postural driving assessments. Both areas are of high importance to employers affected by working days lost through illness.

Over time Maria's healing instincts have grown stronger, both in the medical and spiritual sense. She has always been interested in exploring innovations to help her clients. This has led her to adopt the use of the technological breakthrough of cold light laser treatment for soft tissue sprains, injuries or helping post-operative wounds to heal quicker and minimise scarring. The cold laser works by photonic stimuli, generated by the laser to infuse the body's cells with energy that reduces inflammation, encourage cell regeneration, and increases blood flow.

Strength of spirit often defies conventional medical logic. Maria never underestimates the healing power of the soul in her work. She has studied FLP (Future Life Progression) as a path to learning more about the interconnectedness of the physical and spiritual elements of healing. FLP techniques produce a deep sense of relaxation that often proves beneficial to ease stress, soothe the mind, and signposts a positive life-path to the future.

Parting Points

Maria wanted to pass on these final thoughts as you consider your future business life:

- In business, as in normal life, people connect with people, so try to become the person you always wanted to be physically, emotionally and spiritually.

- When her father, Bill Morris, was very ill, he never gave up. Even towards the end, he wanted to be taken out from the hospital ward to feel the wind on his face, to feel alive. So, try to keep the pressures of running a business in perspective, make time for yourself, recharge your batteries and maintain the balance in your personal life.
- Be cautious about entering a business partnership. Get the agreement in writing. Have an exit plan and keep things amicable before any recriminations start.
- One alternative to entering into a partnership is to remain separate, work in collaboration with others and agree an SLA (Service Level Agreement). This will preserve your financial independence and give you control over personal decision making.
- Never over-promise and under-deliver.

Maria Morris
M: 07787 532 586
maria28morris@googlemail.co.uk

**Business Services
Personal Trainer**

Stuart Amory
Personal Fitness Instructor

"Personal fitness is not just a physical thing. My aim is to help bring about a positive long lasting change in the way people think about themselves, by getting their physical self-image and mental self-esteem in kilter."

Key Advice

- You need to be confident of your own abilities. Project that confidence to those around you, in a reassuring but not egotistical manner
- Put in the time to learn as much about your chosen field as possible and strive to be the best you can be
- Listen to advice from mentors and consider what they say, both praise and criticism, to help you decide on the right path for you
- Create a fresh new perspective in your business to stand out from the crowd
- Be open to luck. Recognise and take advantage of an opportunity when it comes along , and go with it to where it leads

Background

Stuart joined the Royal Air Force in 1995 as a physical training instructor. After four years, he was chosen to train as a parachute jumping instructor, to work alongside the Parachute Regiment, Royal Marines and the SAS. From 2003 to 2005, Stuart was part of the world famous RAF Falcons parachute display team.

Stuart left the RAF in September 2005, and gained a diploma in personal training and sports massage with Premier International.

The Personal Approach

Stuart's military training, combined with the PR (public relations) role he performed as a member of the Falcons display team, was excellent preparation for life after the RAF. He could now use his physical training techniques and inter-personal skills to forge his own vision of the future. Stuart has always adopted a very holistic approach, believing you need to change minds as well as bodies to achieve the ultimate aim of sustained personal fitness.

Another important element in his success is Stuart's strong entrepreneurial drive. He could have taken the safe option and joined a health and leisure company, but instead chose to develop his own special brand of health and fitness programmes.

Open to Opportunity

By chance, Stuart saw an advertisement from the BBC Blue Peter programme looking for guest presenters. He applied and sent a video in support of his application. He didn't get the job, but did get an hour-long phone conversation of encouragement from the producer. The next time Blue Peter needed the services of a personal trainer, Stuart got the call.

This one opportunity has led to his fitness programmes being used by Zoe Salmon, Emily Blunt, Beth Cordingly, Jenni Falconer, Gethin Jones and Sir Trevor McDonald, to name but a few.

Fast Forward to Today

Stuart has now appointed two expert trainers to work with In-Kilter to widen their geographical reach. As a great believer in fresh air, In-Kilter hold regular keep fit boot-camps in local parks. Activities include kettlebells, boxercise, circuits, resistance training, Nordic walking, TRX training, and a variety of other exercises designed to promote fat loss and create lean muscle tissue. Personal training in groups or for individuals complete the In-Kilter itinerary.

The Power of Social Media – Facebook-Twitter & YouTube

It'll come as no surprise that a business so dependent on word-of-mouth has embraced social media as a valuable tool to build business. Facebook and Twitter have provided a hugely effective personal broadcast media channel to attract new clients and motivate existing ones. The frequent posting of YouTube videos on these sites, effectively reinforce training and dietary messages, and is a proven way to strengthen relationships by giving praise and encouragement. The results speak for themselves. Stuart now has over 2,300 followers on Twitter, and as a direct result has been invited to Manchester to give a kettlebell class to a group of keen Twitter followers.

Parting Points

These parting points have particular relevance if you're involved with promoting your personal talents.

- Build your confidence by developing skills and knowledge.

- If you're pitching for business, put yourself in your prospective client's shoes. What is it that they're looking for and how can you be of real value to them.
- Think of a business pitch or presentation as a performance. Rehearse and rehearse until you are fluent, anticipate awkward questions and prepare responses.
- Whatever you may feel inside, when you're working you must make people believe that you are the answer to their needs.
- Build a team of advisors that you can trust.
- Create a genuine connection with the people you work with. Show tolerance and understanding in stressful situations.
- Be generous in your praise and share what you've learned. In business your credibility is enhanced by being prepared to pass on what you know, but don't give it all away!

In-Kilter Fitness
T: 0778 844 8520
stuart@inkilterfitness.co.uk
www.inkilterfitness.co.uk

Trade Services
Plastering

Kevin Ring - Plasterhawks

"You've got to treat every single job, big or small, with the same high level of professionalism. My business has been built on customer satisfaction and the personal referrals that come from continually doing a good job."

Key Advice

- Learn the trade. Get your NVQ qualifications in whatever skill you decide to enter. Practice, practice, practice until you're ready to go it alone.
- Never underestimate the power of a good word. Gather testimonials where you can. A happy customer will tell other people about you. This is the surest way to get new customers and keep in work.
- Be professional in your dealings and remember that you're a guest in someone's home, clean as you go. This is a real pain in the plastering game, due to the mess the powder makes, but it's got to be done.

- Don't rest on your laurels if you're having a good run of jobs. Continue to promote yourself as much as you can. You don't want to be left with nothing in the book if the work dries up.
- Be flexible. Take small jobs as they get your name around and lead to bigger things.
- When you start, think about creating a business name that fits with your trade and gives people confidence. It will allow you to expand in the future as you grow from a one-man-band.
- Placing an advert in the local paper worked for me. I also have my own website and have joined a business networking group.

Background

Kevin used to work for BT (British Telecom). It was an internal job sorting equipment. It was solid but monotonous and without a great deal of job satisfaction. At home, he was having some work done on a new extension. The job had reached the plastering stage. Kevin was pleased with the result, and having watched the plasterer at work he decided he would like to join the plastering trade.

He took some holiday time while still working at BT to attend an intensive 5-day training course. This was followed by a further 10 months of friends and family asking him to do various plastering jobs in his spare time to develop his skills. Then opportunity knocked. BT on a cost-cutting drive asked if anyone was interested in taking voluntary redundancy. A family conference followed. If BT offered enough to pay the mortgage and keep the family afloat for a full year, then plastering would take over from sorting equipment as his new day job.

The Launch of Plasterhawks

A plaster hawk is the square metal tray that holds the plaster before being applied to walls. The name appealed to Kevin. It was a bit quirky and linked nicely to his new venture. He invested in a white van and found a website that printed self-adhesive signage. Kevin parted with just £70 to get a brand new identity and advertise his services.

That was in 2003. As soon as he could, he gained his NVQ (National Vocational Qualification) in plastering. Kevin was fortunate in his timing as he established and strengthened his business in the years that followed before the current economic downturn.

During those early years, Kevin joined a business networking group that produced some excellent business referrals. These referrals contributed 30% of his total business income. Furthermore, joining the group gave him the chance to talk about business issues with other people and get specialist help, including the design, build, and hosting of his new website, www.plasterhawks.co.uk.

Opportunity Knocks Again

At an early stage, Kevin decided to target private residential homes rather than working for less money on building sites. While plastering is still the mainstay of his working week, he had another one of those experiences where watching someone else at work gave him the idea. This time it was damp proofing.

On the basis that when a new damp course is injected, the old plaster is removed and replaced with new plaster, a link with the whole process made perfect sense. Kevin trained to become qualified in chemical damp course injection. Using his woodworking skills for replacement skirting, he has now extended his services and earning opportunities.

Parting Points

- Make it a priority to look after yourself when you're on the tools. Protect your hands, knees and eyes if you're in the plastering trade, as the lime in the powder can irritate the skin. Look after yourself physically whatever trade you're in.
- Listen and learn from others, even if you're doing things better than them. It's still a valuable learning experience to improve your skills.
- Strive to be as good as you can be, with training and relevant qualifications.
- Spend time building relationships with customers – if they like you they'll recommend you. Be reliable and don't turn up late.
- Always be alert to opportunities to extend your income earning potential, linked to your core business.
- Don't be afraid to quote a higher price, if you can demonstrate the better quality or value of what you're doing.

Kevin Ring
Plasterhawks
M: 07984 690 796 T: 01784 457 471
plasterhawks@yahoo.co.uk
www.plasterhawks.co.uk

Popular Start-Up Options
6
Buying an Existing Business

Here are two approaches to buying an existing business.

1. Become involved with your chosen going concern as a part-time employee – paid or unpaid. The nature and level of involvement could depend on your skills, experience and degree of financial contribution.

   This is a stepping stone approach before purchase and you'll get to know the business intimately before you commit. It will highlight the strengths and weaknesses before you invest.

2. Buy an existing business outright and take total management control.

Working within a company before you make any financial commitment will provide vital research and on-the-job experience. What appears to be a healthy profitable organisation from the outside may reveal a different, more sobering picture from the inside.

If the company and prospects are looking attractive, the due diligence process begins. Due diligence is a term widely used to cover all those financial and legal aspects, that deliver hard evidence to help you reach a decision whether or not to proceed. Due diligence is a process you'll encounter throughout your business life, in the normal course of business. You'd be wise to conduct due diligence research to establish facts and credentials before taking any action, especially if you are working with a supplier or trade customer for the first time.

Due diligence involved with buying a business may include:

1. Learning who the legal owners of the business are and what is their shareholding position in the business.

2. Looking back over the company balance sheets and past trading record of the company, to include the commitment to current shareholders

3. Checking the current performance of the business to include, sales, volume turnover, profit, liquid and fixed assets.

4. Assessing the current financial performance, cash flow problems, debts and the bank balance.

5. Exploring the legal title of assets, including premises and land, if freehold or leasehold, plus any outstanding leases or hire purchase agreements on machinery and equipment.

6. Checking the local government planning situation. You don't want to buy a business only to find that severe planning restrictions will limit growth potential, or if a construction project or new road development is being planned that will dramatically affect your decision.

7. Researching similar businesses to see how they are run and how they market themselves.

8. Considering how your chosen company has adapted to the demands of change. Businesses have to anticipate and prepare for developments in the marketplace or fall behind.

9. Assessing the existing employee situation for both senior and other members of the workforce including, employment contracts, company pension plans, notice periods, and the total wage bill.

Buying an Existing Business
A Franchise Resale

Ray Thomas
Chemex Swindon

Ray in dark suit, with Melvin Lusty Chairman of Chemex

"When buying a business, check and recheck your due diligence. There's always something that you miss. Something that's not apparent when you first start negotiations. Don't rush. Take your time to understand the business you're buying into."

Key Advice

- Choose a business that relates to your commercial experience and business skills.
- Buying a franchise resale has a number of benefits. Two of these are the training and support you'll receive from the franchisor: another is acquiring a going concern with an existing customer base.
- Get the latest trading figures to see how the business is performing and whether any circumstances have changed since the business was first valued for sale.
- Check the customer base to check for the number of active and dormant accounts.

- Examine the customer profile to see how the business is spread between accounts. If the business is reliant on one or two accounts, the loss of these accounts will dramatically damage your future income.
- If possible, agree a hand-over period in which the previous owner introduces you to the client base and explains the back-office systems and day-to-day running of the business.
- Make a generous provision for working capital to cover running costs, and keep an extra financial contingency for the unexpected.

Background

Ray trained as a mechanical engineer. The disciplines he learned gave him a career-long ability to marshal his thinking and develop his analytical and organisational abilities. His outgoing personality and communication skills came into play as he moved into sales. Over time, he became a regional manager with a multinational company, firstly responsible for the South West region, then extending his territory across to Wales and up as far as Birmingham.

As demands upon him increased, without a commensurate increase in his salary package, Ray started to explore opportunities where he and his family would receive a greater return for his efforts by becoming his own boss. He investigated a number of different business avenues and narrowed the options down to franchising. The question was whether to start from scratch with a virgin franchise territory or to buy an existing operation.

The Franchise Route

As Ray had experience of the motor trade, at one time being the sales manager of a chain of car dealerships, he examined a franchise involved with supplying garage workshops with tools, and another, specialising in bodywork repairs. He also explored franchises that were related to his more recent experience in the health and safety and personal protection equipment (PPE) sector. Finally, he chose Chemex, a business-to-business (B2B) franchise that specialises in the supply and servicing of cleaning and hygiene products.

The Chemex head office volunteered two start-up territories within reach of his Swindon base, and one resale franchise in Swindon (his home town). Buying a resale franchise meant a higher investment but gave him a fully functioning business with an existing clientele and an established reputation.

The Purchase Negotiations

Ray contacted the existing franchisee and spent a day with him to find out more about his territory and customers. The franchisee wanted the business to be transferred to someone who would manage the business well and look after his existing customer base. He'd decided to emigrate to France as part of his own life plan.

On closer inspection, Ray saw that the business had been losing sales and turnover had slumped in the last year. Another worrying aspect came to light. One customer was responsible for 50% of sales. If that customer withdrew his business from Chemex, the whole financial picture would change dramatically. These important factors demanded a revaluation and price renegotiation.

A revised price was agreed and, on 26th April 2010, at the age of 60, Ray Thomas became a business owner. A new, exciting but challenging chapter in his life had begun.

Parting Points

Ray's experience is especially helpful as his business has yet to complete its first trading year. Looking back, he would like to share these thoughts with you:

- Don't let optimism overshadow your better judgement when buying a business. There are always things that are not immediately evident when first getting to grips with a business, not because they've been deliberately hidden, but more to do with your unfamiliarity with the operation.
- Try to identify the pitfalls. Get expert help to review the company's trading record and customer base.
- Examine in fine detail the basis of any goodwill attributed to the company. Remember that people buy people. It's potentially dangerous to buy a business that has been built mainly on the personality of the incumbent owner. When the business changes hands, customers may not want to keep their business with you.
- Never rest on your laurels. Look for new business every day. It is inevitable that, for one reason or another, you'll lose customers. You need to bring in fresh business to compensate for business lost.
- Make sure you over-deliver on the quality of service you provide. You may not be able to compete on price these days, but an attentive, professional service not only wins business but builds customer loyalty. You've heard the saying that some people "know the price of everything, but the value of nothing". Due to cost pressures, customers do switch to get a better financial deal, but often return when they realise they've forfeited quality, reliability and product performance.

- Create a financial buffer to fund unexpected costs. For example, the rise in diesel prices has hit our van delivery costs. Unexpected events are another reason why you should grow your sales from existing customers and, put time aside to contact and win new customers.

Ray Thomas
T: 01793 771901
M: 07949 704931
www.chemexfranchises.co.uk/Swindon

Popular Start-Up Options
7
Starting a Business with a New Product

Horse before the Cart

The horse is your new product. The cart is the business you've set up to exploit the potential of your idea. I've stated the obvious, as it's the invention, development and testing of the product that comes first, as it will be the generator of wealth to drive the business forward.

Taking the step of establishing a business is your vote of confidence in the demand for the product, its growth prospects and financial returns you expect. The most important aspect is getting a genuine indication of the level of demand for your concept. Many people pursue a new product idea only to find there's no demand for it. Time, effort and money are wasted as a result.

First Things First

The process of creating a new product stems from either a bolt of inspiration or an exciting development on an existing theme that outperforms current products.
The inventions of television, the telephone or the electric light bulb are inspired. Apple Computer's iPad, Trevor Baylis's hand-wound radio, Sir James Dyson's Airblade™ cold air

hand dryer are technological advances that create a stunning new reality.

The Process of New Product Development

At one point in my career, I was involved with companies who had established brands in the marketplace. Their marketing departments and R&D (research and development) were tasked with finding the next successful product based on their known production and marketing capabilities. These companies had the advantage of already having a starting point of knowing a great deal about their products and consumer attitudes toward them. They knew about likes and dislikes, price sensitivity, and the age and gender of users.

A gap analysis was conducted to identify groups of consumers who were not using their range of products. A new product would be created to appeal to those consumers utilising the manufacturing resources already available.

Even though these were multinational companies, the principles are the same as a one-man-band wanting to launch a new idea. These are the staging points in the process:

1. Research

Conduct desk and online research to evaluate the current state of the market and identify any close competitors. If there are similar products available, check these elements:
- Price: How does it compare with yours?
- Packaging: Product names, colouration, image
- Positioning: Who is the product aimed at? Age/gender/socio-economic group?
- Product quality: How does it compare with yours?
- Promotion: How is it being advertised?

- Place: Where is the product on-sale? How it is being distributed to the trade and to consumers?

2. Product Development

How will you differentiate your product from others? Consider these aspects:

- The product quality and the combination of ingredients
- Colour, smell, taste, feel of the product or outer packaging
- Product performance – will it last longer/ is it more technically advanced/ is it more flexible or easier to use? What are the product benefits?
- Design of container – bottle shape and size

3. Market Testing and Customer Research

Conduct market research to validate your concept and indicate improvements:

- Carry out suitable tests on product performance and customers acceptability – your customer may be members of the trade and/or the general public
- Get reactions to a choice of product names to see if you have a clear winner
- Suggest different price points to get consumer reactions
- Check packaging ideas – size/shape of containers. Don't forget to leave space for bar codes and any legal information requirements
- Consider the dimensions and design of the shipping container to transport the product to the customer.

4. Sales Tests

Organise a test market to test trade and consumer reaction:

- Produce product samples and offer them on a sale-or-return basis to suitable local outlets
- Open an online shop to test reactions and to see if your product is suitable for mail order

5. Preparing to Launch

Finalise your product presentation, price and costs:

- Calculate the minimum product sales forecast
- Confirm production estimates
- Gather testimonials from your test market and consumer research participants
- Prepare sales presenters and product display units

6. Proposition Protection

Explore the most appropriate way to protect your concept:

- Patent protection, if the idea is totally original and has essential design specifications.
- Apply for a trade mark. You do not have to be a limited company to register a product trade mark.
- Consider registering the company name if you choose to become a UK limited company, only limited companies can register a business name with Companies House. See, www.companieshouse.gov.uk
- Register the design if your product is derivative of an existing type of product – i.e. an improvement on another - see: www.ipo.gov.uk/design
- Register an internet domain name to capture the name for your forthcoming website

Spanish Rings
Spanish-Style Flower Pot Holders

"Many new product ideas fall at the first fence. Beware of chasing your dream and continuing to invest if you're not reaching your sales and income targets."

Key Advice

- Start small. Test your product. Listen to feedback and make improvements before making any major investment.
- Prepare sample quantities to test in commercial situations.
- Spend time developing the product presentation to reach a professional standard of design and packaging.
- Think carefully about targeting your product. Adopt a style of presentation that would appeal to your potential customers.

- Check the price of similar products in your sector. Decide on your pricing policy whether to undercut competitors, match them, or charge a premium price.
- Having set your recommended retail price, calculate your trade prices and volume discount structure.
- Consider offering your product to distributors on a sale-or-return basis to gauge customer demand and trade reactions.
- Obtain at least three quotes from manufacturers, who are prepared to produce an initial low-volume order.
- Begin a round of promotions to carry out performance tests and allow people to sample your products. Take note of their positive reactions for future publicity, and negative reactions, to help fine-tune your product.
- If your product is well received, prepare a press release and send samples to relevant TV programmes and magazines.
- Check the re-supply times from suppliers, if your product takes-off, you will need to know how long it will take to re-stock.
- Double check your product name or newly created brand name. Make sure you are not adopting a name already in use by another company.

Background

In Spain, there's a tradition of hanging flowerpots, metal tins and weird shaped containers on patio walls and balconies. I visited local garden centres to create the same effect, but all I found were holders of twisted wire that had no strength and would not hold anything heavier than a plastic pot.

Frustrated, I designed a flower pot holder that was to become a 'Wall Ring'. A metal workshop produced a prototype to take a 4" diameter flowerpot. The prototype had an 'A' shaped hook with angled legs to hold the pot securely against a wall.

I was encouraged by the prospect of creating a new gardening product of wide appeal and with no direct competition. I decided on the name Spanish Rings, with the idea of creating a name that people would ask for and avoid being seen as a commodity.

1999- Lift-Off

Spanish Rings were test-marketed in local independent garden centres, with me selling directly to the centre managers on a sale-or-return basis. The name Spanish Rings became a registered trade mark and the design was protected through the trade mark office.

In September 1999, Spanish Rings won the Garden Centre New Product of the Year Award at the Four Oaks Trade Show. The next year, I managed to place a set of Spanish Rings into the hands of Alan Titchmarsh at the BBC Gardeners World Live Show at the National Exhibition Centre in Birmingham. Two weeks later, the TV programme, BBC Ground Force, got in touch. When the programme was aired, Spanish Rings went from 25 garden centres to 75 garden centres in 6 weeks! We ran out of stock twice.

Range Extension and Export Sales

At the Royal Horticulture Society (RHS) Hampton Court Flower Show in 2001, people started to ask whether we had a Spanish Ring design to fit a balcony, on trellis or to hide horrible drainpipes. Designs were developed to stay true to the original single pot concept. We gradually introduced Rings to suit all these different uses, and extended the range of sizes and colours.

Because the idea could decorate a patio wall, transform a blank trellis or empty balcony in moments, Spanish Rings caught the imagination and gained popularity. So much so, that with the help and guidance of Gardenex, the specialist

UK gardening export marketing organisation, Spanish Rings was introduced to the United States of America through a mail order catalogue company based in Vermont.

In the following years, Spanish Rings were sold to garden centre groups and mail order companies in Canada, the East and West Coasts of America, Australia, Sweden, France and Germany.

A sister product called Water Rings was introduced and won the Silver Award in the 2004 UK Gardening Awards. Water Rings are a breakthrough in water conservation for plant containers. The product holds a layer of superfast absorbent gel sandwiched between two layers of capillary matting. Water penetrates the matting, expanding the gel and forming an oasis inside the compost, to nourish plant roots and produce the full blooms, especially if a liquid feed is used.

Online Mail Order – A New Way Forward

The growth of the internet has led to a shift in the selling emphasis. The cost of supplying garden centres became uneconomic. Spanish Rings had a retail price starting at £3 per ring. Garden centres expected to receive a 50% trade margin, plus free delivery and free display stands. This did not make commercial sense to us. The more profitable solution was mail order.

If you take a look at www.spanishrings.com you'll see the variety of types of Spanish Rings and prices now available. From a commercial viewpoint, the mail-order route removes the cost burden of garden centres while allowing us to offer a door-to-door service to customers all around the world.

Parting Points

- Take it step-by-step. Test and develop a product proposition that will deliver the volume you need to cover costs and make a profit
- A healthy profit margin is all well and good, but without generating volume you will be directing energies inefficiently.
- Provide an outstanding service to customers, with a quality product that justifies its price point.
- Create a product or brand identity that adds value to your proposition.
- Develop attractive eye-catching designs to appeal to your target market.

STEP 2

The 4 Factors of Start-Up Success

The *4 Factors of Start-Up Success* highlight the key questions you'll have to satisfy before starting a new business.

Once you have the answers, you'll be well-prepared for a successful launch. At this stage, you should have a clear idea about the kind of business you want to set up. Step1 was devoted to the most important factor - **The Human Factor**.

The next two factors of start-up success are:
Factor 2 - The Marketing Factor
Factor 3 – The Financial Factor

Factor 2 – The Marketing Factor
Is there sufficient demand for your intended product or service?

Ask yourself:

- Will people want to buy what you want to sell?
- What is your USP (unique selling point)? The USP is the unique element that makes your concept stand out and be attractively different to customers
- Have you undertaken a gap analysis to identify the business opportunity? (An explanation of a gap analysis follows in the pages below.)
- Is there sufficient demand to make your proposition commercially viable and pay you a living wage?
- Have your researched your market and competitors?
- What is your route to market? How will you distribute your product or service?
- How will you package and present your idea?

- If you've got a retail concept, how will you decide on the location of your premises?

A Definition of Marketing

Marketing has been defined by the Chartered Institute of Marketing as:

"The management process responsible for identifying, anticipating and satisfying customer requirements profitably."

In other words, marketing is the process of producing goods or services that people want to buy, and are profitable to produce. Marketing firstly finds out what people want, then proceeding to meet those needs by designing, creating, manufacturing and selling a product at a profit. In times past, manufacturers would sell the products their factories and machines were capable of making, rather than first seeing what people wanted. Marketing puts people first in the thought process.

In the first instance, market research is carried out to determine what people want. The manufacturer or service provider will then develop an answer to fulfil the need. This may be an improved version of something people already use, for example, liquid washing machine detergents rather than big box detergent powders, or the invention of totally new answers to problems and desires.

Sir James Dyson used his scientific and entrepreneurial skills to develop the bagless vacuum cleaner, an invention that overcame the problem of loss of suction in conventional models, when the inner bag is full of dust.

What is Niche Marketing?

Marketing accepts that we're all different but that we
 tend to fall into particular consumer groupings. In the 70s and
80s, market researchers categorised people alphabetically by
social and economic class. A and B grades were the top
echelon of society - the highest earners. The vast majority of
society made up the C category which was divided into C1
and C2. C1 were professional and management class and
earning above the national average. C2s were well-off, but
lower middle class. Ds were the working class and average to
lower wage earners (cash wages paid in brown envelopes).
Es were the poor or retired. People were further sub-divided
by age, gender and location. This led to more specific
sections of the population being targeted, for instance: C2
women aged 25-35 living in Manchester.

Today, things are a little more sophisticated. Niche marketing
is a refinement that seeks to meet the demands of much
smaller and more discerning groups of people. A product
may be aimed at pre-teens, or mothers with toddlers, or fans
of classic cars, or people who don't eat products with gluten
in them. You get the idea. The name for this process is niche
market segmentation.

From the financial viewpoint, even though a niche market
may be small, the returns can be considerable. If you supply a
quality product that is hugely attractive to an affluent sub-
group it, can be extremely profitable.

Gap Analysis

A gap analysis examines two things, customers and
competition. A business may identify a gap in the market. The
gap being an unfulfilled consumer need that a company has
the expertise and capacity to satisfy. Any gap presents an
opportunity if competitors are not already active in that area.

Discovering a new and lucrative market segment creates a clear commercial advantage.

For example, Esure Insurance spotted a gap for car insurance aimed specifically at women. Sheila's Wheels was created to target women drivers and fulfil that need.
Conducting your own gap analysis is a useful way to test if anyone else is doing the same thing that you plan to do. Don't be downhearted if there is. Your ideas may be an improvement, with an extra benefit to consumers. By researching the market you can learn a great deal about products that are already available, their price and presentation.

If an idea is totally original this could be a lucrative opportunity. Or playing devil's advocate, it may be that there is no interest and no demand for it. By doing a gap analysis, you'll find this out sooner rather than later, and before you commit a huge amount of time and money.

Introducing 5 Marketing 'P's
1.Product 2.Positioning 3.Place 4.Presentation 5.Promotion

1. Product (or Service)

The process for launching a product for sale or providing a service is fundamentally the same. To begin, you need to consider whether you can make a living out of what you want to do. In short, you need to calculate whether there's sufficient demand to sell a sufficient quantity to make enough profit to meet your income targets.

If the answers to this set of questions are honest (and not wishful thinking) you could be on to something.
Ask yourself:

1. Is your idea fresh, original, and attractive?

2. If it's based on an existing concept already on the market, what makes it special and different. How will you gain an edge over competition?

3. Has your concept got mass-market potential or is it a speciality purchase for a niche market?

4. Could the product start small but have the potential to grow into a mass market product?

5. Have you researched the market to identify the competition

6. Have you conducted a gap analysis to pinpoint any missing opportunity your product can dominate? You may have spotted something missing in terms of what consumers may want or your product may have features which are different and attractive.

7. Have you researched the market potential? How are players already in the marketplace performing?

8. Is the market subject to rapid change – for example, with seasonal highs and lows or changing fashion trends?

9. Is your product a one-off or can you add other related products over time to create a range with strength in depth?

10. Is your product easily copied? If it is, it will be.

11. Do you need intellectual property protection, copyright, patent protection or design protection?

12. If creating a totally new and innovative product, what control do you have over production? It's wise to explore different suppliers, get quotes and create fall-back positions if someone lets you down.

13. If it's a retail venture, are there any established patterns you can improve upon? For example, vary your opening days and times to capture the greatest number of customers.
14. If providing a service, can you be flexible in terms of meeting times? Could you arrange to see clients in their homes or offices?

15. If offering a product, what level of after-sales service will you offer?

16. How price sensitive is the market? Sometimes just a few pennies can be enough for consumers to leave your product and buy another.

Practical Research to Help Answer These Questions

Sitting at your computer using the search engines to explore domestic and international markets is a given when starting your research. Help via the internet is there in abundance. Clicking from website to website will produce a wealth of information and help you perfect your concept.

You can also employ practical techniques to gather information and strengthen your proposition. It's surprising what you can find out simply by talking to people if you become a secret shopper. Secret shopping is the tactic of visiting a shop or a competitor in the guise of a private customer and asking questions to learn about:

- Product prices and range members
- Packaging styles
- Product attributes
- Promotional activity – type and frequency
- Personal service – style and attentiveness of staff
- Presentation and in-store display

- Professional opinions from sales people working for other companies in your field.
- Other products on the market and get feedback. Both good and bad reactions are valuable.

2. Positioning

Positioning is a vital exercise. Positioning determines how your product fits into the marketplace in terms of its basic business proposition and who it will appeal to.

First, look at the competitive marketplace. This may be on a local, national or international level and assess the opportunity for your concept.

As you do this, you'll build a picture of the marketplace and learn:

1. Who are your closest competitors?
2. What are their prices?
3. What exactly is their product offering? What do they do that attracts custom?
4. About how they promote themselves, locally, regionally or nationally?
5. How popular and what is the demand for their product?
6. Whether the market segment they occupy is big enough and profitable enough to accommodate more entrants
7. Whether the market already too crowded, with cut-throat competition centred on price and price alone? (a dangerous situation)
8. The importance of sales location – high street, city centre, retail outlet, conventional mail order or internet web-based operation.

A. Identifying Your Core Customer and Prime Target Market

Age, gender, attitude, ethnicity, fashion, influences, likes/dislikes, habits, entertainment, family connections, holidays and travel, earning power.

These are just some of the different elements of consumer demographics and psychographics. By combining these two elements, you can build a pretty accurate profile of your likely customer and their lifestyle. Some businesses find it helpful to create a visual mood board of photos and lifestyle images, cut from glossy magazines in an attempt to represent the characteristics of their customers.

You could also create a number of different customer categories. These can be subdivided according to their frequency of purchase, number of visits or purchasing spend. They might be further classified as heavy, medium, or light buyers of your product.

B. How to Create a Unique Selling Plus

A unique selling plus (shortened to 'USP') goes to the heart of your idea and is the essence of your proposition.

Your USP is the strength of your product or service that will:

- Make you stand out
- Make you special
- Provide the key element of excitement and interest which your target market finds appealing and wants to buy into

If you target key buyers accurately, you can design your company image and message to have the greatest appeal. This could involve using visuals and developing a particular tone of voice in your communications which are more likely to attract attention. Let's face it, we all have so much going on in our lives, it is up to the start-up business to create a total offering which cuts through all the busy static and gets you noticed.

3. Place – Your Route or Routes to Market

Take a large sheet of paper and some coloured pens. In the centre draw a circle and in the middle of the circle write either Me, My Product, My Service, or My Shop. Then, add two boxes at the top of page one marked B2B the other B2C.

B2B stands for 'business-to-business' and B2C for 'business-to-consumer'.

Depending on the nature of your business you could be selling to other businesses, directly to members of the public, or quite often to both. For example, an accountant may have both private clients and represent businesses at the same time. It is part of the planning process to decide where best to direct your energies to achieve the greatest return.

If you've got an online business, you could well be selling to anyone in the world. My point is that you can explore different avenues or different routes to market to suit your chosen product or service. You may have a high street shop to sell directly to the public, sell over the internet and also supply a wholesaler to distribute your goods to other trade customers up and down the country, as well as supply mail order catalogue companies.

Here's a list of direct and indirect selling opportunities. When planning your business, you can take advantage of any number of ways to sell and in any combination.

A. Direct routes to sell to the general public, either singly or by combining several selling channels:

1. From a high street shop
2. Online
3. At shows and exhibitions
4. From your own mail order printed catalogue
5. Selling off-page with advertisements in newspapers and magazines
6. Through direct sales to people in their homes
7. To people invited to product parties, e.g. jewellery, cosmetics, fashion
8. Direct to trade customers. An example would be a baker supplying direct to hotels and restaurants

B. Indirect Routes to the Trade or General Public:

1. Via wholesalers
2. Mail order companies – conventional printed catalogues or via internet mail order
3. Export trade customers
4. Distributors and licensees
5. Via concessionaires

Pick up those pens again, and draw lines from the B2B or B2C boxes to the matching distribution paths both direct and indirect routes. This will create a diagram of selling opportunities and potential income streams. As your pen makes the last connection, it will give greater form and substance to your business vision.

4. Presentation

Business Names, Product Names and Trademarks

Giving your enterprise a name, even if it's only a temporary working title, will bring your project to life. Striking the right note, that reflects the function of your business and matches the product or service, is the beginning of creating a strong company or brand identity.

Creating a new and unique brand identity is a valuable company asset. The brand becomes the umbrella under which other associated products can be launched. Trademarks are the visual representation of a product identity further adding value to the brand proposition.

Here are three of the most common naming routes:

1. Named after a real person – the founder or creator of the venture. Examples include: Alan Michael Sugar Trading (Amstrad), Michael Dell (Dell Computers), Sir James Dyson (Dyson), Clarence Birdseye (Birds Eye Foods).

2. Descriptive names linked to function: British Airways, Easy Jet, Capital Radio.

3. Brand names stemming from a product: Coca Cola, Nike, Castrol, Amazon, Google, Microsoft

In Britain, it is not possible to register a business name unless you are a limited company or limited liability partnership.

To clarify, trademark rules are different. Any business or individual can apply to register a trade mark.

Checking a Business Name

If you intend to operate as a sole trader, you can use your own name or decide to create a different name for your business. It's best to check to see if anyone local to you uses the same name as yours. It may be best to avoid the danger of any misunderstandings and choose another trading name.

Companies House is a valuable resource to make sure your chosen name does not infringe regulations by using proscribed words or unauthorised use of protected names or abbreviations. For more information, visit Companies House at www.companieshouse.gov.uk

For trademarks, copyright, patents and designs protection visit the Intellectual Property Office: www.ipo.gov.uk

Trademarks are an expression of brand identity - a visual signature that triggers an immediate link to the brand. In the commercial world, trademarks are literally a stamp of quality to differentiate one product from another.

Importantly, as graphic symbols, they do not directly describe the goods or services in their design. For example, the symbol for Marks and Spencer, the famous high street clothing and food shop is - Your M & S. The logo style does not refer to what is sold in their shops. Their trademark is the identity that runs through all their communication, online and offline, to make the company stand apart from their competition and be instantly recognisable.

Big Mac, and Whopper, are trademarked names. The Mickey Mouse cartoon and the Golden Arches are in turn, trademarked symbols of Disney and of McDonald's. As with the M & S example, they do not directly mention the company's products, but by using the symbols on all their publicity, websites and stationery the symbols are intrinsically linked to the organisation, the ® or ™ symbols are used to identify the trade mark as their protected property.

Company Identity and Graphic Design

It's worth briefing a professional graphic designer to prepare some outline visuals of your business name and symbol for you to consider. Get at least three versions and develop the one you like most. Smart, attractive designs say a great deal about you and your business.

These are mistakes to avoid when designing your company business cards:

- Using tiny script that is too small to read
- Forgetting to say what your company does
- Forgetting to say exactly what you do
- Forgetting to give your name sufficient prominence
- Using a weird non-standard size and shape that will not fit into a wallet, purse or business card case
- Overlooking essential contact details including landline numbers, mobile phones, email or website URLs
- Covering your card in a kind of plastic coating that will not allow anyone to write on the card. Business contacts often like to write the details of where they met you, along with the date and if they have to set up a meeting
- Not using the reverse of the card at all. If you put your contact details on the front, use the back to describe your products or services.

Website Development and Social Media

From a functional viewpoint, there are two types of website. 'Brochure' sites are those with little or no evident presence on the World Wide Web. By this, I mean that unless you are in the possession of a web address or enter the correct company name into the search engine, the website will not be found. It will be practically invisible to search engine robots.

The second type has been optimised in order that search engines will locate your website. SEO is the speciality that enhances a website with elements that will be registered by the robots and feature you on Google pages. This means that information embedded into the site will help your site be recognised, using:

1. Key words or phrases that relate to the nature of your business or products. These words are emphasised repeatedly within your website and included in areas that only search engines visit.
2. Tags and metatags are descriptive words added to a web page that help define the nature of your site.
3. Keywords in the title of each web page – called <title> tags.
4. Links to other websites, in order that visitors to those websites follow the link and arrive at your website.
5. Backlinks that are created by the use of blogs, writing articles or social media. If you publish a blog or article or sign up for a social media site, your URL will create a link back to your own website.
6. Postings on YouTube videos or podcasts on your site that link to the Google search engine, via a free account you can set up with YouTube. A podcast is an audio recording you download from the internet.
7. PPC (pay per click) is a way to promote your website for cash. You pay an agreed sum to Google each time a visitor 'clicks' on your site.
8. Submissions to search engine directories, for example, Google, Bing, and Yahoo, and sponsored business directories, such as bttradespace.com and thomsonlocal.com

For more information on SEO, visit www.optimisemywebsite.co.uk or www.thesmallbusinessseocompany.co.uk

5. Promotion

It's vital that in conjunction with your plans to start the commercial wheels turning, you spend time to thinking about how to get those wheels turning faster, and get your business off the ground quicker.

In parallel with any product-related sales promotion ideas, you need to think about how you can constructively promote yourself and your business. This is why I want to talk about social media and business networking. They're essential tools for a new business.

Social Media – Personal and Business

A social network used by private individuals or businesses is an online internet based tool that promotes interaction between a person posting a message and another responding. This allows 1-2-1 communication or between groups of people.

Facebook and Twitter can be used for both private and business interplay. ecademy and Linkedin are business-based organisations that can raise your profile and connect you with relevant interest groups of people you have worked with or would like to work with in the future.

The social media concept is based on the spirit of sharing information. Advice is freely shared in the belief that by giving out you will receive back, either in terms of gaining credibility or gaining new business referrals.

There's a difference between a business lead and a business referral. A lead is just the contact details of a business that may be a new prospect for you without any kind of personal testimonial involved. It may be just a name and number – no more.

On the other hand, a business referral is where someone believes that you have the skills to provide a professional service. This involves someone having trust and confidence in you. They are giving you the contact and a personal reference at the same time. This is a referral.

Business Networking

Business referrals are the currency of networking.

Becoming an active business networker produces these benefits it:

- Provides the opportunity to promote your business
- Increases confidence in public speaking
- Raises your personal profile and builds trust
- Is a forum to ask for advice from other small businesses
- Delivers concrete business gains, by receiving good quality referrals
- Creates your own business network of specialists who can help your business grow, by meeting people like accountants, tax specialists, solicitors, sales and marketing specialists, graphic designers, printers and business coaches
- Connects you with people who can help you in your private life, for example trade services like builders, decorators, electricians, plasterers, plumbers and garden landscapers

There are networking meetings that you can attend for free, just search for local business networking events online. Check out your local Chamber of Commerce who will hold networking events to raise your profile.

There is nothing to stop you attending these and other networking meetings *before* your business starts to trade.

I guarantee you will be greeted warmly, and gain valuable free advice and guidance. Visit at least a couple of networking groups before you decide which one to join. Any group should ideally have a balanced mixture of both trade and professional members.

Promoting Yourself

If you decide to go along to a business networking meeting, you will be asked to introduce yourself. At first, this can be daunting, especially as you may be given just one minute to do it. This guide is to help you discipline your thinking and put across the points you want to make. With practice you'll be fine and be able to speak with confidence.

How to Write an Effective 60 second Business Pitch

If you're at a networking event or in any business situation, you will have the chance to make a great first impression. But, what do you say to promote yourself and your business?

60 seconds is all you've got. The question is how long is 60 Seconds? The answer is between approximately 160 and 200 words, depending on the speed of delivery.

Knowing the approximate number of words you can speak in a given time, will allow you to think of time in terms of parcels or segments of facts and information. You can break down time into bite-size chunks and craft your message into an effective mini-presentation. One of the great benefits of presenting a so called elevator pitch is that it requires you to prepare an accurate and objective assessment of your business, and the benefits it will bring to a new customer. It's a good discipline.

The 60 Second Template – A Guide to Successful Business Speed Pitching.

You can shape the content and timing to fit your message. This guide is to get you started by writing down what you want to say in a structured way. Time yourself, as you speak the words to see how it suits your speed and style of delivery.

Content Suggestions	Seconds	Words
Your name, company name What function do you perform?	10	30
What are the unique selling points? What makes you different?	15	35
What help or advice are you looking for?	20	60
Ask if anyone would be interested in learning more, or arrange a follow-up contact.	10	30
Ask for business cards and give them yours.	5	15
Total:	**60**	**170**

Here are a few business networking groups to explore:

Women in Business Network - wibn.co.uk
The Athena Network - theathenanetwork.com
Chambers of Commerce - britishchambers.org.uk
4 Networking - 4networking.biz
BNI - bni.com

Factor 3 – The Financial Factor
Can you make a sustainable profit in the short term?

Ask yourself:

- What is your price point?
- What is your profit margin?
- What are your sales estimates to calculate profit?
- What are your product costs?
- What are your estimates for set-up and running costs?
- When will you first make, then sustain a profit?
- What will your cash flow provision be?

Negative cash flow kills businesses. This happens when the business runs out of ready cash to meet costs. Often, this is because there are insufficient funds available as a capital investment in the first place, or that money due to the company from sales has not be received in enough time to match money being paid out. The business gets out of balance, pressure from creditors mounts, bills remain unpaid, pressure increases and the business fails. Game over.

Pricing

Undercut. Price-match or charge a premium. What's your pricing strategy? How are you going to determine your prices?

These are the four positioning options when first setting your pricing. Do you:

1. Attract customers by charging a lower price than similar products on the market and continue at a price point below the brand leader?

2. Price-match the brand leader, but offer a short term promotional price discount to encourage consumers to sample the product?

3. Price-match the brand leader and keep the same price without offering a discount

4. Charge a premium price, because your product has advanced features, higher production quality or has some other factor, like a designer label, that gives your product a higher perceived value.

Price Setting: Cost Plus or Price Down?

Here are two methods to calculate the standard selling price of a product. Let me explain the two approaches:

1. Cost Plus

The starting point is to calculate all the costs involved in producing a product or supplying a service. Typical costs are rent, rates, wages, production costs, marketing costs and delivery costs. All costs are totalled and apportioned to the volume of sales expected, in order that every single product sold has a cost allocated against it.

The next stage is to add a percentage profit margin. These two figures added together, plus VAT or sales tax, give the trade price. The trade price, plus a percentage for the wholesaler, and an additional percentage for the retailer margin, produces the final consumer selling price or recommended retail price.

A cost plus scenario is an option if you have a totally new product and have the advantage of setting an original price point. It is also possible to reap the benefit of a cost plus strategy, if you have a strong trading position and an established reputation. If Calvin Klein for example, launches a new perfume, they can set their own price point as leaders in the market.

This is what a cost plus breakdown looks like:

1. Production and sales costs	Assume £2.00
2. Profit margin. Allow 100%	**Assume £2.00**
3. Net trade price	£4.00
4. VAT on trade price @ 20%	0.80p
5. Total trade price	£4.80
6. Assume 100% trade margin	£4.80 = £9.60
7. VAT @ 20% on retail price	£1.92
8. Total retail price	**£11.52**

2. Price Down

For this example, let's assume the decision has been taken to price-match the brand leader, who is selling at £11.00. Being the brand leader with a higher sales volume, it's safe to assume that their costs per item are less than ours, which will have an impact on our profit margin, as it is costing us more to trade.

8. Retail price of brand leader	**£11.00**
7. VAT – 20% of £11.00	£1.83
6. Total trade price	£9.17
5. 100% trade margin	£4.59
4. 20% VAT on trade margin	£0.77p
3. Net trade margin	£3.83
2. Costs	£2.00
1. Profit margin	**£1.83 = 92% margin**

In this case, making the decision to match the brand leader has reduced our profit, as our costs have remained the same.

A Word of Warning

There's a great temptation for a new business to set a low price point to get established in a market. Beware. It's easier to come down from a higher price than move up from a lower one. Furthermore, it is essential to generate as much income flowing inwards as possible, so setting a competitive price will deliver greater returns.

The strategy of setting a first price comparable to the brand leader, then negotiating short term price reductions, is more astute and may encourage acceptance and trial by new stockists. Stockists will always be interested in a generous profit margin, especially if it's greater than they usually get.

Low Price = Low Quality. Right or Wrong?

When it comes to pricing psychology, you may be surprised to learn that offering a low competitive price is not always a good idea. If people expect to pay a premium price, let them pay it to protect your product image. If you're making a substantial profit, smile all the way to the bank.

As you will appreciate, it often takes time to build a strong product and brand identity, and achieve the on-going benefits of gaining the confidence and trust of customers. This is why so much importance is given to creating a strong brand identity.

Profit Margin vs. Volume Sales

It stands to reason that the lower the price, the higher sales volume you'll need to cover costs and make a profit. Mass market grocery products, like baked beans, make pennies in profit but the volume is immense.

If you operate in a niche market, your pricing model may deliver a large profit margin from small volume sales. It all depends on what the market will stand and the perceived value of what you have to sell.

With Spanish Rings, I offer a special promotional price at flower shows; customers can choose any three Rings for £10.

I have to sell 100 sets a day to make £1,000, that's about one sale every 5 minutes of selling time. Last year, a talented artist at the RHS Hampton Court Palace flower show, sold 2 sculptures at £950 each, covering his fixed costs on the first evening.

However, he was fortunate that evening, and sold comparatively little in the following days. At the end of the show, the gap between us had narrowed, as a result of the greater volume I had sold.

Freelancer Pricing

If you're a freelancer, you need to be as flexible as rubber. Depending whether the client is a large or small company, the size of their budget, and the nature of the job, you'll need to pitch your fees at a suitably competitive level.

Having said that, like conventional pricing, you need to work out your monthly costs and calculate how many days you need to work to cover costs at your normal going rate. If your day rate is £300 and monthly costs total £3,000, you need to work for 10 days. That's an accountant's way of looking at time and effort, but it does help you set targets and discipline your working schedule.

Profit - The 3 Different Elements

1. Breakeven

Without making a sustainable profit, a business will fail.

It's true that in the early stages, a business may rely on the financial buffer of working capital, to cover possibly months of trading losses. It is not unusual for a restaurant, for example, to trade for some time at a loss, until it becomes established and builds a loyal client base. This is why planning is such an aid to managing your finances, especially if you take a realistic view to avoid disappointment.

The point where it moves from the red into the black is called the breakeven point and income exceeds costs. We will revisit breakeven points in Step 3.

It's all part of understanding the need for making a financial provision to meet start-up and trading costs for the first months, not forgetting a separate fund to meet your personal and private spending needs. The important thing is to plan and make a sufficiently large allocation of money, (working capital), to see you through to the breakeven point and beyond.

2. Gross Profit

Profit is the difference between total income earned and costs. Gross profit is the result of any one transaction, where the total income received is set against the direct costs of making the sale. The direct costs are those that can be attributed to a particular sale, including production costs, packaging and sales.

The gross profit margin is a percentage calculation between selling prices and direct costs. For example, if you sell a product for £25 with direct costs of £15 you're left with a margin of £10. £10 as a percentage of £25 = 40%. You have a 40% gross profit margin.

3. Net Profit

Net profit is the amount left when you subtract all the other costs of running the business. These are the fixed costs and would include rent, rates, wages and a provision for corporation tax.

The 'net result' is called your bottom line.

Factor 4 - The Planning Factor
Do you have the resources for the first crucial months?

The business plan will provide a benchmark for everyone involved in running the business and demonstrate your talent and capabilities to a bank manager or financial backer, but most importantly to yourself and supporters.

The importance of this first plan for your business will be to:

- Define your business goals, legal status and target market
- Assess the commercial viability of your business – consumer demand, break-even point, estimated first year profit and loss forecast
- Include a financial forecast total income against total costs
- Include a cash flow forecast – estimated timing of income to balance payments with receipts
- Clarify the nature of your business model and its potential in the marketplace
- Anticipate and overcome obstacles
- Confirm your launch strategy and timing plan
- Give a vision of future developments

Step 3 is dedicated to The Planning Factor

The business plan will give you the confidence to turn planning into execution.

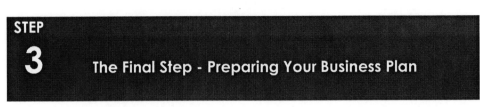

Before we take the last step...

What Does Success Look Like to You?

There's a phrase some business coaches use. They look you straight in the eye and ask:

"Why are you starting a business?"

They wait while you eagerly provide a litany of answers:

- To be my own boss
- To have control over my own destiny
- To make a profit
- To leave the rat race and work when I want to work
- To make a profit
- To realign my work/life balance
- To support my family

And so on...

When you've run out of steam, the coach waits longer than is absolutely necessary and delivers the pearl of wisdom. These three words are spoken crisply and with a voice suddenly increasing in volume with the emphasis on the middle word:

"To sell it"

The words are left hanging in the air, floating in a bubble of silence. The coach takes a breath, smiles benignly and explains. The logic is that no matter what your reasons are for starting a business – whether you're dead-set on global domination or want the business to fund your existing lifestyle, or any point in-between – the business has to be run in such a way to create a valuable asset attractive to a future buyer. Preparing a well-conceived and thoroughly researched description of your business is the start of creating a most valuable asset.

Introducing
The Business Plan
Welcome to the business plan. Your plan to make money.

The business plan is your battle plan. It marshals all your resources and directs them to achieving your objectives. Preparing your first business plan is a practical demonstration that your chosen business route will not only make money, but enough money to cover costs and generate funds, to not only get you going but keep you going.

All the reading, thinking, planning and preparation you've done will give you the confidence that you've got it right before you start.

Reality is waiting for you. Reality has the habit of not doing what you expect it to do. This is where a plan will help you navigate your first 12 months and minimise (but not eradicate) surprises. Life would be dull without surprises. That's why your business plan cannot be set in solid concrete.

You must be responsive to lessons learned and be prepared to make changes. The business plan is your route map to the future. Don't worry if you take a wrong turning here and there - we've all done it. Just get back on course and avoid being side-tracked.

Don't, whatever you do, beat yourself up. Remain positive.

Preparing Your Plan

These are the central elements in your business plan.

1. A full and thorough description of your business venture and business name
2. A market review and description of your place within the market and profile of competitors
3. Your first year marketing plan
4. Pricing, sales forecast and break-even point
5. Financial forecasts, income and cash flow to include start-up costs and working capital requirement to include details personal budget provision to keep your head above water.
6. State the chosen legal identity i.e. self-employed, sole trader, partnership, limited liability partnership, limited company (see below for information on all these different types)
7. Personal profiles and related experience of key personnel
8. Management Summary

A management summary is the last thing you write, but the first to be read. The role of the management summary is to be a straightforward introduction to the business for bank managers, investors, or friends and family to provide a digestible overview of the business.

The following pages will look at 4 subject areas of writing a business plan in more detail. These are:

1. The legal identity of a business – sole trader, partnership, limited company
2. Finance and cash flow – profit, break-even and charts
3. Your marketing plan – your launch plan and supporting activity
4. The management summary for the bank or investors and key point recap

1. Business Legal Entities

Sole Trader, Partnerships and Limited Companies

When deciding on a legal status, there's a temptation to opt for either an LLP (limited liability partnership) or limited company, because they seem more credible than starting as a self-employed sole trader.

 LLPs and limited companies do have the provision where partners and company directors limit their personal liabilities to the amount of money they've invested in the business. Should the worst happen and the business falls into receivership or becomes insolvent, their private assets would not be at risk. However, there's far more control over their legal and accounting obligations

In reality, a bank would require personal guarantees on any lending made to a company. This means that directors would be required to pay back any money lent to the company if the company should fail. This is a summary of each type of business entity.

Author's note: The following section provides a general overview. Please seek expert advice for a fuller picture and learn of any recent developments.

1. Sole Trader

Advantages	Drawbacks
Simple to set up. You must inform HM Revenue and Customs (HMRC) of your decision to become self-employed and register with them. See http://www.hmrc.gov.uk/selfemployed	The law sees you and the business as one. You will be personally responsible for all aspects of the business

Trading is uncomplicated. You must keep records for tax purposes and define what purchases are for personal and which are for business use. National insurance contributions are usually lower than limited companies.	Banks may not be willing to lend to a sole trader. If they do, they will require personal guarantees.
Accounting and paperwork is kept to a minimum. You must make provision for your personal tax, national insurance and VAT if you're registered. The threshold for registration is currently a turnover of £70,000 per annum. (This level does change so please check online.) See http://www.hmrc.gov.uk/vat	Should the business fail, you may risk personal bankruptcy.
As a sole trader, you have complete control over the operations of the company and accountancy fees are lower than that of a limited company.	Limited companies are often seen as more secure than sole traders. This could affect your ability at first to get credit from suppliers.
You can change your status and become a limited company once your business model has been proven.	

2. Partnerships

A self-employed partnership has the same obligations and liabilities as a sole trader.

Advantages	Drawbacks
Partnerships are simple to set up. You'll be classed as self-employed for tax and national insurance purposes.	Without a deed of partnership, arguments can occur over profit sharing and salaries.
There is more than one person driving the business forward and responsibilities can be shared, depending on the talents and capabilities of the partners.	All partners are joint and severally liable to losses of the business.
As there are more people involved in the business, there may be a bigger fund of money available to help the business develop.	All partners may be held liable for the actions of any one partner. This can happen if one partner enters into a contract without the agreement or knowledge of fellow partners.
As for sole traders, there's less paperwork and less professional costs as a result.	When there are a number of people involved in a business, there may be different views and disagreements on business operation and future strategy.

3. Limited Liability Partnerships – LLP

Limited liability partnerships are similar to the partnerships mentioned above, save for the fact that partners benefit from limiting their own liability. Another difference is that the LLP is responsible as an entity for the debts of the business rather than individuals. That's unless one or more partners have guaranteed a debt or loan to the business.

The drawback is that the LLPs have to comply with many of the same accounting and legal requirements of a limited company.

4. Limited Company

A limited company has a separate legal identity to the people who've set it up. It exists and can continue to exist in its own right if the original people leave or sell the company. The company usually issues shares to the directors, company secretary and any investors. The officers of the company are not liable for the debts of the company over and above the amount they've put into the it.

A limited company has to have at least one director who may also be the company secretary who is the person responsible for making the necessary returns to Companies House.

Advantages	Drawbacks
Limited liability of shareholders to capital invested in the company. Private assets are protected from debtors unless personal guarantees are given.	The degree of administration required. Filing Annual Returns and submitting company accounts.

Limited company names are registered and protected.	The admin operation of a PAYE system.
Capital can be raised by selling shares in the company.	Reports and annual accounts to be available to Companies House and the general public.
Being a limited company can be an advantage when dealing with suppliers. You are deemed to be less of a risk than sole traders	The cost of professional services to prepare accounts and help manage aspects of the administration.
Employees of the company can receive shares in the company – either given as a reward/bonus or offered for sale at a special price.	The need to give personal guarantees to get loans for the company with banks and other lenders.
If you sell a company you may still have a vested interest in it by holding on to a number of shares – with the agreement of the buyer	Higher tax may be paid by limited companies

2. Finance and Cash Flow

Sales Forecasting and Breakeven

If you're starting a business from scratch, you will not have any past sales figures on which to base your future sales. Assuming you're in a complete void, with no idea of what to expect, you have no choice but to total all your costs and fix your prices then calculate your gross profit margin, to estimate your breakeven point over the coming 12 months.

Calculating the Breakeven Point

To calculate your breakeven point before you get accurate figures from actual monthly sales you've achieved, you divide the gross profit figure into costs. This gives the number of sales you need to make to reach the point of break-even.

 Like this:

Assume you have product costs of £10,000 per year. Your gross margin is 40%. You divide the £10,000 by 40% x100 = £25,000 = 100% of income required to break-even.

Out of the break-even point of £25,000 (100% total income) 40% = £10,000 covers the direct product costs and 60% = £15,000 covers the other overheads to run the business.

Put another way, as your profit margin is only 40% (not a full100%) you need to sell enough to make up the missing 60% it takes to run the business which is £15,000 + £10,000 = £25,000

Monthly Sales needed to Breakeven

Using the example above, you'll need a sales target of £4,167 to break-even after 6 months or £2,084 over 12 months. Clearly, as soon as you reach breakeven you move into profit before tax.

This example is designed to demonstrate the principle of calculating the breakeven point. Life is never this simple, as there will probably have a number of different products on sale at different prices. Consequently, they will each have different gross profit percentages. The way round this is to find an average gross margin percentage and apply that to the cost figure.

Sales Profile, Seasonality and Start-Up Timing

Toy shops make the largest percentage of their sales in the run-up to Christmas. DIY companies can't wait for Spring. Ice cream companies love the Summer. You know where I'm going with this... If your business has a marked seasonality, it makes sense to plan your new business launch in time to maximise the seasonal returns. Get ready and prepare any premises, stock and online marketing to capitalise on the period of maximum returns.

Review your sales profile to spot the periods of sales uplift and be ready to pounce with a promotion to generate the highest returns for your marketing.

Cash flow Dynamics and Working Capital

Personally, I think there's a danger that the words cash flow can evoke a serene scene with money flowing out and money flowing in like some gentle river of commerce. Not a bit of it. Cash flow should be named 'cash lag' as you'll need all your skills to manage the time-lag between making a sale and getting paid. People who've bought your product or service want to hold onto payment – that is in effect your money - as long as they possibly can.

The whole purpose of making sufficient provision for working capital is to have funds available to bridge the gap between making a sale and receiving the cash. It's a fact that most small businesses are undercapitalised in this respect. Don't let it be you.

I cannot stress enough the importance of having access to enough working capital before you start trading. If you start on a shoestring budget, the first unexpected demand and you may be forced to take another line of credit, or get an expensive business loan that you can ill afford.

It is one thing to apply a break-even calculation across a 12-month period as we've just done. It's quite another to receive income from customers or business clients in the same reliable and structured way.

In reality, companies will take 60 to 90 days to pay you. You'll have a 30 day credit standard but you'll be very lucky to get paid by everyone in that time period. If you work on a 45-day receipt basis, this should build in enough leeway in your cash flow planning.

Not only that: when you start your suppliers will expect you to pay them either upfront or within 7 to 30 days. If you don't, they may refuse to deal with you again. When people get to know you, then things will ease up a bit. The only practical way of handling the situation is to chase people who owe you money and create a cash flow fighting fund that will keep you solvent.

Cash flow Tip. Plan your purchases to Synchronise Payments with Receipts

You need to keep a strict eye on purchases and don't be tempted to buy anything until you absolutely need to. This is called just-in- time ordering and minimises your exposure. Remember, it's your money that people are spending when they are not paying you. This is business, and being nice has to be applied when tact and sensitivity is needed. If someone is being awkward and not paying, that's when you say: "no more Mr/Ms/Mrs Nice Guy!"

Sales and Cash flow Model

How to complete a cash flow forecast during pre-start.

1. First, concentrate on estimating your pre-start costs. Then set them against the starting capital input from your private funds and any contribution from family or other sources.

2. Divide the total capital figure into three parts. One is to pay for fixed start-up costs. The second is a provision for working capital. The third is your personal subsistence fund to keep you afloat.

3. Costs will broadly fall into two categories – fixed and variable costs. Fixed costs, as the name suggests, are those known and recurring costs that do not vary a great deal. For example, rent, rates, wages, loan repayments, lighting, heating, and leasing costs.

4. Variable costs are those linked to sales, like the cost of stock, marketing, packaging, delivery, telephone, travel and vehicle expenses including petrol and diesel. These costs are called variable because they are a function of how busy, productive and successful you are. The busier you are, the more sales, the greater the costs that need to be set against the increased sales you're achieving.

5. Once you've got an idea of costs, you can place these against the prices you intend to charge and work out the gross profit. From that figure, you can calculate your break-even point and the amount of sales you have to achieve each month to reach breakeven.

6. Knowing the monthly sales figure you have to reach, you can estimate the split between cash and credit sales. This will depend on the trading nature of your business: if you're running a sandwich bar, most sales will be cash, with only a small proportion of corporate clients paying on a credit account. On the other hand, if you are a freelancer you'll invoice after a job has been completed and hope to be paid in 30 or 60 days, depending on the policy of your client.

   For cash sales, write the figure in the actual month of sale. For credit sales write the income figure a clear month *after* the estimated sale date.

Sales Forecast and Cash flow Chart

As the days and weeks go by, you'll be able to monitor income and outgoings accurately. At the end of each month, you can alter the estimated figures in your original cash flow chart to the actual amounts. The earlier you spot any dramatic under- or overestimate the better. If sales are not performing you can quickly move to make the necessary changes and consider sales promotion or other marketing support techniques. If costs are ballooning out of shape, you can review the price you're paying for goods and services, and perhaps hire or fire suppliers in order to achieve the level of service you require. Don't sit back because you've just started in business; speak to suppliers and shop around for more cost effective or more reliable people to work with.

The charts on the next few pages show a quarterly picture of sales and cash flow. They will help you complete a quarterly income and expenses picture where A = Income and B = Expenditure.

A = Income

Income Source	Pre-Start	Month 1	Month 2	Month 3	Month 4	Total
Cash Sales						
Credit Sales						
Owner Capital						
Working Capital						
Other Income						
Total A Income						

B = Expenditure

Expenses	Pre-Start	Month 1	Month 2	Month 3	Month 4	Total
Cash Purchases						
Credit Purchases						
Rent and Rates						
Tax and N.I.						
Repairs and Fittings						

Drawings					
Phone					
Gas and Electricity					
Travel					
Marketing					
Stationery					
Capital Purchases					
Advisor Fees					
Bank Charges					
Total B Costs					
Net Cash Flow **A minus B**					
Balance Brought Forward					
Closing Balance					

Add different cost boxes to suit your type of business. The items above are to give you the general idea of cost centres to set against income received.

The intention behind this model is for you to identify different sources of income and plot a spending pattern. It's likely that before start-up, you'll face one-off charges that will not re-occur, for example professional and legal fees involved in setting up the business and perhaps the artwork, design and print of business cards and stationery, as well as marketing costs involved with buying a domain name and having a basic website built.

The first time you complete a spreadsheet like this, you will be taking money from the starting capital of the business to pay for set-up charges before you begin to trade. Then, as far as you can, complete the other sales and expenditure figures having estimated your gross profit and break-even figures. This will show you how much you'll need in reserve as working capital.

And...don't forget to create a personal survival fund to keep you alive, before you can afford to take money from the business.

Business Plan Subject Detail

3. The Market and Marketing Plan

Sun Tzu, a Chinese military strategist from the sixth century BC, wrote the influential book titled The Art of War. In the book there's a chapter: Know Yourself – Know your Opponent. As you prepare to write your own business battle plan you will need to demonstrate that you have a good understanding of your own business vision, and how it relates to the marketplace and your competitors.

There's a tool used to identify characteristics and develop marketing strategies. It's called a SWOT analysis and this is what it looks like:

A SWOT Analysis	Write your answers in these spaces
S – What are your **STRENGTHS**	
W – Identify your **WEAKNESSES**	
O – Explore your **OPPORTUNITES**	
T – What are your **THREATS**	

Look in the Mirror

A SWOT analysis is used to turn a mirror upon yourself and your business plans, to honestly examine where you have strengths and identify any weaknesses. Fundamentally, this is a positive exercise as it highlights skills that we may need to learn ourselves, or gain from someone else, with a complementary set of skills, to supplement our own. The process can be enlightening, especially when you get to the opportunities and threats sections, where you embrace forward planning and think beyond the start-up period, to the future expansion and growth of your business.

In today's market, the threats section can be a life saver. If you're involved in the latest technology and selling a gadget that is currently the state of the art, it will inevitably be outmoded leaving you behind if you don't embrace 'the next big thing'.

The overall lesson is to understand that all businesses have to adapt quickly to changing trading patterns and consumer needs. Change is ever-present and it's how you anticipate and adapt to change that makes you stay the course. Look at the rock star re-inventions of David Bowie or Madonna to underscore this point – they've kept relevant to their market as you must do with yours. Tony Mingoia of the Palazzo restaurant has a strategy of updating and changing his menu and surroundings on a regular basis, to anticipate and fulfil the changing tastes and demands of his customers. That's one reason he's survived.

The SWOT Competition Examination

Putting your competitors under the microscope, using the SWOT technique, is a learning experience for you and anyone reading your business plan.

Using the Strengths–Weaknesses–Opportunities-Threats matrix, you will quickly determine what competitors are doing well and expose weaknesses to exploit.

For the purposes of the business plan, research the local market to see:

- Whether there are similar competitive businesses in your locality. If so, how are you different? For example, can you offer a better, more flexible service, or alter your opening hours to suit the habits of your customers.
- If they targeting the same type of customers as you.
- Where their premises are located. Does this give them a competitive advantage?
- If there's a big enough demand to sustain your business in your chosen locality?

Looking Outwards with a PEST Analysis

A SWOT analysis concentrates very much on the current immediate market position. If your business is aimed at wider export or technological fields, then a PEST analysis that stands for (Political – Economic – Social – Technological) factors, may be one to include in your business plan. It will, once again, demonstrate your understanding of external issues that may affect your business and impress the reader.

Turn the page to see the chart template.

A PEST Analysis	Write your answers in these spaces
P Are there any **political** issues that may affect your business for good or for bad?	
E Are there any wider **economic** issues that may shape your approach or present opportunities?	
S Are there any **social** or community matters to be wary of or embrace?	
T Are there any changes or developments in **technology** that should concern/excite you?	

Demonstrating knowledge of the market and your competition will only positively reinforce confidence in your own business proposition. Knowing your opponent and understanding their business model only makes yours stronger and more persuasive to banks and backers.

The next task is to decide how to unveil your new business

The Launch Plan. Slow Burn or Fireworks Display?

The Slow Burn Approach

You can opt for a Slow Burn launch on a low marketing budget that:

1. Allows you time to overcome any early teething problems

2. Gives you the opportunity to see that you've got the business mix correct

3. Puts money in the bank as you start to trade

The slow burn strategy can be a pragmatic way of getting established and without spending a great deal of money. You can limit your marketing spend to:

- Getting business cards designed and printed
- Joining local business networking groups
- Registering with online networking and social media groups such as Twitter, Facebook and Linkedin
- Getting listed in local business directories for example, The Best Of network or ones zoned by county, such as networkinginsurrey.co.uk

As the weeks go by, you can crank up your advertising and marketing and invest in a website to expand your activity. When you're certain that you've got all the ingredients right you can plan a fireworks display.

A Fireworks Display

By this, I mean a concerted campaign to get you noticed and promoted within your locality.

This could involve:

- An actual launch event with invitations to other local businesses and influential contacts, including the local media
- Local advertising and editorial space in your local newspaper
- A launch promotion to attract new customers and encourage repeat business
- Investing in a website
- Starting an email marketing campaign and producing a regular newsletter

On-going Marketing Support

As the dust settles over the launch phase, you'll have the opportunity to assess how well your activity has been received and shape your on-going marketing plans. It may be that you develop plans aimed at different types of consumers, with the key objectives of:

- Continuing to attract new customers
- Maintaining the loyalty of existing customers

If you've bought into a going concern, there's a third group to target...

- Reactivating lapsed customers.

Marketing Campaign Planning

Here's a structure that will help your planning and create a disciplined approach to preparing your marketing plans. By adopting a structure, it will become a reference point for you to assess and set a benchmark for the future.

The chart suggests a logical progression of elements to adopt as a template.

1. Background	5. Timing
2. Objectives	6. Budget
3. Strategy	7. Post Activity Analysis
4. Target Market	

Point by point

Background
The background sets the scene for the activity. It may highlight a changing trading situation or an opportunity you've identified to benefit the business.

Objectives
The objectives are statements of what this activity is designed to achieve. The more specific and measurable the objectives are the better the post-activity analysis.

Strategy
The strategy explains how the objectives will be achieved and what specific action is to be taken – either affecting price, introducing a sales promotion or mounting an advertising or PR campaign

Target Market
This identifies the group or groups of people you aim to influence with the activity you plan to run. The target market should be identified as accurately as possible to make the activity focused and relevant

Timing

When the promotional activity will run and how long will it last. Will the activity be planned to coincide with a period of high demand or with a particular event, school holiday, or special date in the calendar?

Budget

This will outline the money available to pay for any advertising or promotional material, and to support the promotion and for any direct cost of any sales incentive.

Post Activity Analysis

Gather the results of any activity and compare them with the original objectives. This will help you learn lessons in advance of the next campaign. It's a great idea to speak and get feedback from customers while the promotion/activity is going on.

4. Writing the Business Plan Management Summary

The management summary should be no longer than 2 pages. The job of the summary is to give an overview of your business plans and communicate the key points, but leave the detail to the supporting sections. The tone, and to some extent the content, will vary depending on who you're writing it for.

If you have all the finances in place, and the business plan is primarily for your management purposes then your first business plan will provide the benchmark for future achievements.

If on the other hand, you're writing to attract a potential investor or for a bank manager, the aim is to make them:

1. Excited by the idea and your ability to make it work
2. Impressed with your depth of knowledge of the market and the competition

3. Confident of your personal business background and management talent
4. Reassured of your people-management skills
5. In agreement with your financial assessment and the method you've used to calculate the future business prospects
6. Stimulated by your marketing ideas and sales support strategy
7. Greatly encouraged by your profit forecast
8. Approving of the amount of money you're asking for and what you intend to spend it on
9. Supportive of your projections that will lead to an exit strategy for the investor (remember words of the business coach – "the only reason you start a business is to sell it")
10. Appreciative of the personal investment you are contributing as your stake in the business
11. Accepting of the percentage share in the business you have proposed in return for the financial backing

If you're writing to get a bank loan, then the emphasis should be place on the strength of the business concept and your ability to generate a sufficient commercial profit. Expect any lender to ask for personal guarantees for any money lent to you, and further to ask for another person of substance to act as your guarantor.

Last but certainly not least, writing a business plan will give you confidence that you're on the right track. Your business plan will reflect one moment in time, the time it was written. The first plan is immensely valuable but should be refined and updated by events. Don't stick to it like glue. Improve and develop the plan as circumstances change. Continue to build on the strong foundations you've created.

Key Point Recap

As a reminder, here's a repeat of the business plan contents.

- Define your business goals, legal status and target market.

- Assess the commercial viability of your business – consumer demand, break-even point, estimated year one profit and loss forecast.

- Include a financial forecast of total income against total costs.

- Include a cash flow forecast with estimated timings of income and expenditure.

- State the nature of your business model and its profit potential in the marketplace.

- Anticipate and prepare answers to potential criticisms

- Confirm your launch strategy and timing plan

- Describe your vision of future growth and development for the business.

Parting Points

Here are two final pieces of advice learned over the years.

1. Problem Solving

Cutting Problems Down to Size

When a problem seems overwhelming, deconstruct it. Cut it down to size. If you reduce a problem to its separate elements it's much easier to cope with. The big problem gets into perspective and easier to handle. This is called the Russian doll solution, where a big outer doll holds smaller dolls, each one diminishing in size until you find a tiny doll at the end.

Something tiny you can master, you solve the big problem by reducing it to its component parts.

If you're dealing with something you have no experience of, speak to someone who possesses that valuable experience. They'll help you find the answer. You may be able to help them solve something troubling them in the future.

2. Prioritise

Direct your Energies Efficiently

Take a pen and piece of paper, and write down a list of *everything* you have to do in connection with the business (and in your private life, if you wish) in any order. At this stage, don't assign any priority ranking to the list.

Once all the things you have to do are put down, sort the list into two parts: matters that are important and matters that are urgent.

Important items are those which have a high value or great worth to you.

Urgent items are those driven purely by time pressures.

Often, the two aspects coincide, or you may decide that something which is important has to wait until a smaller urgent matter receives your attention – but that's life, you will at least have imposed some order on the chaos of pressure and stress.
It may help to grade your priority list by matters that are:
1.   Very important and very urgent
2.   Quite important and urgent
3.   Urgent in descending order of time
4.   Not important and not urgent, but needs to be done at some time

If you do this, your time will be managed both effectively and efficiently.

Signing Off

The aim of this book has been to extend a helpful welcome to the world of business from fellow travellers.

Personally, I've made more mistakes in my career than I care to remember - mistakes that, at the time seemed stupid or downright dangerous.

You'll make mistakes too.

I hope, as do all the other generous people who've shared their experiences hope, that as a result of reading this, your mistakes are containable, won't keep you awake at night or break the bank. Seeking help and advice is always a good policy.

Success Before Start-Up will raise issues that require further reading and investigation. There are many talented writers who'll supply the answers.

The good news is that now, you'll know the right questions to ask.

If you'd like to get in touch, visit www.startuptosuccess.co.uk

Thank you.

Start-Up Success -Year One. The Next Book

Success Before Start-Up concentrates on the vital period before you start trading. The next book in the series *Start-Up Success - Year One* examines all the practical issues of getting your business up and running for a successful first year.

It will lay the groundwork for success, by providing guidance on marketing and finance, including raising funds from conventional lenders, business angels and venture capitalists.

Start-Up Success - Year One will again feature contributions from small businesses who will describe their first year experiences. Additionally, we will interview a range of specialists who provide essential professional support to new businesses. They will explain how their input will help a young business flourish.

Fast Track Your Business Writing Skills

Improving your personal communication skills is money in the bank. *Fast Track Your Business Writing Skills* is a straightforward guide to developing content, style and structure to your business writing. By improving these skills, you will become a better communicator and more able to express your ideas, discipline the decision-making process and influence others to drive your business further forward.

Importantly, the book will focus on the three watchwords of business writing:

1. Purpose: be clear about what you want to achieve.

2. Clarity: use simple, well-structured arguments to communicate clearly.

3. Brevity: get to the point quickly and don't pad-out proposals. Your aim is to swiftly inform and gain acceptance of your plans to reach your goals.

Fast Track Your Business Writing Skills will develop not only your writing skills, but your thought and preparation processes as well. These benefits will soon become apparent in building confidence when speaking to groups of people. The book describes the three main business personality types that form your readership or audience, and explains how to address them to best effect.

About the Author

Steve Bridger

Steve started his marketing communications career in advertising with Young & Rubicam (Y&R London) before joining Collett Dickenson Pearce (CDP). He gained sales promotion experience with Mike Leeves Promotions and won the ITMA Gold Award for Sales Promotion.

Steve created a new product and established a start-up business in the gardening market - Spanish Rings Limited. Spanish Rings are Spanish-style flowerpot holders.

Spanish Rings won the Garden Centre New Product of the Year Award. The company website was a finalist for Website of the Year. Water Rings, a new product launch from Spanish Rings, won a Silver Award in the UK National Gardening Awards. Spanish Rings went on to be sold in Canada, the USA, Australia, UK and Europe.

Steve spent five years in the music business, first as a spotlight operator and lighting crew member. He then worked with the band 'Mungo Jerry' (In the Summertime was their Number One smash hit) and visited Poland, Denmark, Germany, Bulgaria and Zimbabwe. He was with the band when they played at the opening of the Jebel Ali Club in Dubai.

Following the Jebel Ali gig, he set up 'Debut Entertainment Agency' and took entertainers out to the UAE for three years.

Steve has sailed the Atlantic Ocean as a member of a delivery crew aboard the yacht Blackfin from Gibraltar to Antigua.

He attended the RAF Changi Grammar School in Singapore.

Today, Steve's experience is channeled as a freelance marketing communications consultant, copywriter, and director of Spanish Rings Limited.

Please visit:
www.startuptosuccess.co.uk www.thewritecopy.co.uk
www.spanishrings.com.

Lightning Source UK Ltd.
Milton Keynes UK

172822UK00001B/80/P